Surviving Schizophrenia:
A Memoir

Louise Gillett

Published by Twynham Press
Paperback 2nd edition

ISBN 095669373-0

Twynham Press

With love

CONTENTS

FOREWORD

What you are about to read is a true story. I am a middle-class mother of four children. I look and behave as you might expect a person of my age and stage of life to look and behave.

However, at the age of nineteen I was diagnosed with schizophrenia. I felt a deep sense of shame and embarrassment about this and tried to keep it secret for many years, even after it became clear that the label was erroneous.

I agonised for a long time over whether to make my story public. I wrote this book, re-wrote it, changed the names, changed them back again. I wrote it again under a pseudonym, then tried to change it into a novel. Then finally, in 1999, on a writing holiday at the wonderful Arvon Centre in Totleigh Barton, Devon, matters became clear. This is my story, and I am ready to stand by it. It is a true story and any value that it has for others lies in that fact.

1
St Ann's Hospital, Poole

I woke alone, in a large room. It was empty except for the mattress upon which I lay, fully dressed, and a commode. There was no bedding on the mattress. I strained to look around. My vision was blurred, and I thought first of my contact lenses. On other occasions over the last few years I'd found myself waking up in strange places, and at these times I worried about the health of my eyes.

This felt different. This was nothing like when I'd crashed out, drunk or stoned or both, at friends' houses or music festivals. I quickly realised that it didn't matter whether I was still wearing my contact lenses or not. It was more important to find out where on earth I was.

The room was painted white. The surfaces of the walls were uneven, and the paint was chipped in places. There were three tall, wide windows across one side of the room, reinforced with a smeary layer of secondary glazing. On the wall opposite the windows was a heavy wooden door, plain and ugly, at odds with the elegant proportions of the room. The top panel of the door was glazed, but I could see nothing through the glass because a blind was drawn over it. The door was closed and the blind was on the other side.

I stood up with difficulty. How long, I wondered, had I been lying there? I felt dizzy, faint and very thirsty. I walked unsteadily to the tall windows and looked out. What I saw made me more confused, rather than less. The size of the room, and the beautifully landscaped gardens, said 'stately home'. But the décor and furnishings, or lack of them, shouted something else. I knew instinctively that if I could put my finger on what that was, I would solve the mystery of where I was.

I glanced down at my clothes. Strange. Every item I was wearing belonged to my sister, Jane. I loved my own clothes. I'd worked hard and saved to buy a collection of cherished items, most of them from French Connection. My sister, on the other hand, had a six-month-old baby and still carried some of the weight she'd gained in pregnancy. Her brown cords and old, black jumper hung unflatteringly from my thin frame. My head ached. What was going on? What had happened to me, and why?

I made it across the room but found that the door was locked. I hammered on it loudly, calling out for help, for water. Meanwhile, my mind was still turning the problem over and the mists had begun to clear. By the time a pleasant-looking, middle-aged woman appeared with a plastic beaker of water, I didn't need to see her nurse's uniform to help me work it out.

I took the water over to the mattress, where I sat to drink it. The nurse stared down at me. 'Do you know your name?' she asked. 'The date? And where you are?'

'I'm Louise Gillett,' I said. 'It's the 14th of April, 1988. And I'm in St Ann's Hospital, in Poole.'
In the loony bin. But I'd remembered the date. Surely that must prove I was sane. I felt very small and scared, but at least I was lucid.

2
I Am a Writer!

My certainty of my own sanity did not last long. As I started to remember the series of events that had brought me to the hospital, my mind shied away from the embarrassment and shame of it all. *The loony bin.* I began to panic again. I knew I'd been sectioned and that this had happened at my sister's flat. I'd been staying with Jane, her husband and their baby during my Easter break from university. While I was there my mental state had deteriorated rapidly and when I was taken to St Ann's I had become totally incoherent. In other words, I was raving mad.

The last thing I remembered from my old life, the one where I was, if not fully sane, not yet officially insane, was being in Jane's bedroom with a GP who administered an injection, a shot in my arm. I'd seen many different doctors in the previous few days, some of whom I didn't know at all, but I recognised this particular GP from my local surgery.

Today, more than thirty years later, I still cringe to remember that I thought this man was, in fact, God. I believed he was giving me a lethal injection to release me from all the confusion and unhappiness. He was very handsome, as befitted his exalted role in the Universe, although I did think it was strange that he smiled when I addressed him as God. Surely the good Lord could not be laughing at me? I decided it must mean that my advent to Heaven was a happy occasion, and so I gave myself up willingly to whatever drug was in the syringe.

It must have been a strong sedative, because the next thing I was aware of was waking in that bare hospital room. After asking for a drink and getting one, and then finding that, however painful my recent memories were, at least I was in touch with reality, I was confident that things would improve.

But over the next few hours, all that happened was that a succession of medical professionals appeared in the room at intervals, asking the same questions. 'Do you know who you are? Where you are?'

I gave the same reply each time. 'Yes, I am Louise Gillett and I am in St Ann's Hospital in Poole.' After a while, I became tired and confused. There seemed to be no chance of progress, no improvement in my circumstances. Perhaps I was giving the wrong answers.

Eventually, the part of my mind that had struggled in vain to understand what was happening to me as madness set in, the part that had switched off to prevent itself from burning out, decided it was time to give up the fight once more. Panic set in, and before long I was babbling again.

I have no memory of anyone making any effort to soothe or comfort me. I felt like a caged animal, and my behaviour mirrored that feeling. I rarely stopped talking from that point onwards, the whole time that I was locked in that room (which I later learned was for 'observation of acute cases'). I refused to take any of the pills that were thrust at me, because I didn't trust anybody who was offering them and I didn't know why I was expected to take them. The result was that I was visited by teams of nurses, four or more at a time, who held me down on the mattress and injected me with drugs. I hadn't realised until then that a lot of nurses in mental hospitals were male, or even that they could be male, and, for me, that fact added to the indignity of the experience.

One morning, I asked a female nurse whether I could wash, and she brought a bowl of water which she laid on the floor. She handed me a flannel. I'd been expecting a bath or shower, and all at once my situation seemed unreal. I'd always had a lot of vivid dreams, often nightmares, and I decided that the only sense to be made of this situation was that it must be a dream. An extended one of course, but then there was never any real sense of time in dreams. I decided to test my theory. I'd throw the water at the nurse and hopefully, the shock of whatever happened next would be enough to wake me up.

I have never been a violent person. I knew that if this wasn't a dream, I would need to check that the water wasn't too hot. I couldn't risk hurting the nurse. I crouched down, dipped a finger in. Lukewarm. Good. I stood up, holding the bowl, and threw the water from it towards the woman. She was drenched. Did I laugh at the horrified look on her face? I am afraid I might have done. So perhaps I only had myself to blame for the events that followed, because of course things got worse after that.

I was kept in that room for many days, and in all that time I had only one visitor from outside the hospital. It was my mother. She perched sadly on the edge of a chair that had been dragged into the room by one of the ever-silent nurses. She was clutching a bunch of flowers upside down as she gazed down at me marooned on my mattress on the floor. She'd never been a communicative person and I didn't usually speak much myself. We stared at each other for a while, neither of us knowing what to say, until eventually I began to talk, filling the silence with desperate, nonsensical pronouncements, until the length of time that constituted a decent hospital visit finally ran out. I clung onto my mother when a nurse told her it was time to leave. She looked anguished and I believe she would have stayed longer if she could have done, but another group of nurses were called to hang on to me and she was ushered away.

One day, shortly after that visit, I discovered that the door to the room in which I was incarcerated was not locked, and I took immediate advantage. It was not a subtle or clever attempt at escape. I dashed out of the front door of the hospital and down the driveway, brandishing a pen above my head and shouting at the top of my voice, 'I am a writer!' I was dragged back by a team of burly, male nurses, and from that point onwards the door to the room was kept firmly locked.

3
The Room

I spent at least a week in the loneliness and squalor of the observation room, being attacked (as I saw it) by groups of nursing staff with syringes, before I made the connection between those attacks and my refusal to accept the drugs in tablet form. I don't know why it took so long for the penny to drop.

Even now, it is not easy to describe how I felt, to recall those unremitting small dramas and the attendant shame. It was the same every time. The desperate effort to run and hide, the unavoidable capture, the struggle towards inevitable submission. The force the nurses used to subdue me, the sense of helplessness I felt as a result. The dawning understanding of how stupid I was, again, to try to get away. And, because I was a hopeless worrier, a dreamer-up of unlikely catastrophic scenarios, a fabricator of non-existent connections, behind all this was the fear that the nurses might think I was, on some level, enjoying the brutality.

Why was I bothering to fight them when I knew I would be forced to surrender? The answer was simple. It was the fear that made me try to run and hide every time one of those teams of nurses came into my room. I was terrified of their use of force and every time they approached me, panic set in. I do not know how many times the pointless chain of events was repeated before eventually I agreed to take the pills. It was a relief when the 'attacks' finally stopped, although I hated taking the pills, vast numbers of them, three or four times a day, different ones every time.

I was still very scared. I felt convinced that I was the subject of a gruesome medical experiment. I was sure the doctors must be as much in the dark as I was about what was wrong with me, and that they were simply trying every medication they had to see whether any of it helped. I was frightened that I would die from all the drugs before they found out how to help me. I hated the pills and how they made me feel – so heavy, so slow – and I wished that the doctors and nurses in this dreadful place would leave me alone. But I now accepted that this was never going to happen, and so I kept swallowing the tablets obediently, avoiding the violence that I knew would start again if I refused.

Since I was finally 'compliant', at least outwardly, I was moved to a dormitory room in Sandbanks Ward, a large, shared space containing two rows of beds. I was shown to my bed, but immediately became upset because it was higher than all the others and I thought this meant that I was being singled out for special treatment. I wanted to make it clear that I was no better than anyone else.

Even without the befuddling effect of all the medication I was not good with words, and I could only tell the nurses that I wanted the bed to be lowered. When I couldn't explain why, they called Dr Patel, the consultant psychiatrist to whose care I was assigned, and the great man himself came into the room and looked around. 'I see what it is,' he said. 'Lower the bed as she wishes.'

The nurses were sullen, giving me sideways looks as they adjusted the bed. They were obviously puzzled by the support I had received from Dr Patel, and I had no words to tell them that I was as confused about it as they were. I liked the doctor, though, and hoped that he would continue miraculously to understand me.

Now that I was in the ward, I was given weekly

appointments with the consultant, but although Dr Patel was kind his manner was distant after that first time. Every meeting we had went the same way. The appointment would begin late, and I would sit silently for several minutes watching Dr Patel read through a pile of medical notes, to remind him who I was perhaps, or to find out what the nurses said I had been doing all week. There were sheaves of notes compiled every day on every patient in that hospital, and we were never allowed to see what was written about us.

When the doctor had finished reading he would ask, politely and considerately, in his heavily accented English, 'How are you today, Louisa?' I would reply with a babble of stream-of-consciousness, begging him to please set me free, to let me leave this awful place. He would look away from my distress as if it upset him too much to witness it, and then nod to the nursing team. This was their signal that my audience was over, and it was time for me to be removed from his august presence. I'd blown it again, and now another grisly week loomed in front of me before our next meeting, my next chance to convince him to let me go.

In the outside world, it was still the Easter holidays. My siblings visited when they had time, but my mother came every single day. She arrived in the late afternoon after she'd finished her shift in the Royal Victoria Hospital in Boscombe, where she was a nursing sister in the Outpatients Department. Mum sat quietly by my side in the hospital lounge, perhaps feeling as lost as I was. She was a constant presence, an always-show. It seemed that she never knew what to say to me, but of course I wouldn't have known how to listen anyway. I was in a personal, private world, completely consumed by my drugged and wandering mind. Abstracted, incapable of rational thought or speech.

4
Insanity and Fear

As time went on, I became able to see outside the confines of my mind a little, and gradually became more conscious of the hospital as a whole. It was a terrifying place. The area known as Sandbanks Ward consisted of a long corridor with various rooms running off it, at the end of which was the one I shared with five other patients. Nearby was a stone-floored bathroom. One day I asked whether I could take a bath, and after some consultation among the nurses it was agreed that this could be permitted. To my surprise, one of the nurses followed me into the bathroom. I ran the bath, undressed and climbed into it, and she positioned herself on a chair near the tap end of the bath, where she had a full view of me.

It had been bad enough having to ask to take a bath, without being supervised throughout the process. The indignity and lack of freedom rankled more than any embarrassment at my nakedness. Since I was a small child, I had looked after my own personal hygiene and, after I was sent to boarding school when I was nine years old, I became more independent. My mother had a laissez-faire attitude when I was growing up, and I'd left home to live alone when I was sixteen, so I wasn't used to being told what I could or couldn't do.

I sat in the deep bath water, staring at the nurse, utterly baffled. When I asked her why she needed to watch me have a bath she said, in an emotionless voice, 'It's in case you hurt yourself.' She gave no further explanation. I told her that I'd been washing myself since I was young and that I was fully capable, even in my current over-medicated state, but she didn't respond.

I'd realised by now that there was no point arguing with the nursing staff, however irrational they seemed, so I continued to wash, consoling myself with the wonderful sensation of being in a bath at last. I have always loved water.

It was only when I asked for a razor to shave my legs and my request was refused, also, 'In case you hurt yourself,' that I realised what she meant. The thought of self-harm had never entered my head, until then.

There was a shabby day room with a television on the ward, although I hardly ever went in there in the early days of my incarceration. Television had bothered me when I was becoming unwell – descending into psychosis, I'd thought I was being sent messages through the thing. Now I avoided it in case this happened again. The room was always full of patients, sitting like zombies in front of the screen or ranting at it unreservedly. I shunned their company, in the same way as I would have stayed clear of myself, if only I could have done.

The day room was also where a half-hearted programme of occupational therapy activities took place. Opposite was the nursing office, where the staff sat behind glass screens, ignoring us. My sister Mandy often advised me to 'speak to the staff, not the other patients' and so I frequently stood forlornly outside the office, hoping someone would notice me, perhaps invite me into this inner sanctum, and start up a friendly conversation. But whenever someone finally opened the door and asked in an exasperated tone what I wanted, I never had any idea what to say to them, and was invariably shooed away. Conversation never was my strong point.

There was another day room at the end of the ward, equally run-down, but in this one were a few comfortable chairs, a pool table and a piano. There were large bay windows at one end with a wooden window-seat, from which was a wonderful view of the hospital gardens tapering down towards the clifftop. I often sat there, passing the time quietly. I was usually alone, but sometimes another patient joined me and then we would sit together in silence, or near-silence.

The room opened onto a veranda and the whole effect would have been astonishingly lovely, if only. If only there were comfortable chairs on the veranda, if only we patients didn't burn so easily in the sun (one of the many side effects of the medication). If only it wasn't a mental hospital.

The door at the end of the ward was half-glazed, heavy, alarmed. Sometimes it was left open and we could come and go freely; at other times the alarm was set and the door was shut and locked, occasionally guarded by a nurse. I never knew exactly why this was, but somehow understood that it wasn't worth asking. There was danger of some kind, either inside or outside the ward. That was enough information.

Opposite Sandbanks Ward was Flaghead Ward, where the hospital dining room was located. One day our ward door was closed, and I was looking through the upper, glazed section into Flaghead, which seemed to be a mirror image of Sandbanks except that their dining room was in the place of our television room.

There were all sorts of sights to be seen in Flaghead Ward through the glass that day, and I stood for a while watching them all, patients dressed in mismatched clothes or dressing gowns, wild-eyed, wild-haired. Many degrees of strangeness. Even the occasional nurse passing through.

I was joined by another patient, a man, older than me, respectably presented. We watched the parade of madness together for a while before he spoke. 'Any minute now,' he said in a bitter tone, 'we'll see a dwarf wearing a scarf on his head.'

I looked at him to see if he was joking, but his face was impassive and so I turned back to the spectacle. And then to my amazement, a man of very short stature appeared in the ward corridor opposite, with a long, blue scarf swaddled tightly around his head and ears. 'How did you know?' I asked the man next to me, but he laughed and walked off.

I wondered what on earth this had been about, but soon gave up on the puzzle. Perhaps it was a show of some sort, put on for our benefit? But why? Had the older man seen the man with the blue scarf before? Was he trying to impress me or freak me out with his prediction? Or had he suggested something completely impossible, outlandish, which I then hallucinated? Was it all a hallucination? I could be sure of nothing and there was nobody I could ask, even if I could find the words with which to voice my questions.

Books were occasionally wheeled into our ward on a trolley. I can't remember their origin. Perhaps they were brought by well-wishers like the WRVS or delivered from another part of the hospital, where the patients were considered well enough behaved to have permanent access to these privileges. I was happy to see these reminders of civilisation and normality but one day, when I picked up a book and tried to read it, I was horrified to realise that I couldn't understand a word.

The print seemed to have separated. The letters

were spread out and I couldn't join them together, couldn't figure out their meaning in my mind. I was really frightened. When I was a young child and had felt so often alone, books had been my mother and father, my friends, my only and constant companions, my comfort. Books were my life. Even in my rebellious teenage years I'd had books to help me and guide me. I might have paid more attention. Still, they were there.

I had learned to read when I was so young that I couldn't remember the process, and since then I'd devoured every book I could get my hands on. But now, suddenly, I couldn't decipher the words on a page. I was worse than a child, I was a baby. Worse than that, I was a baby in a prison. Even worse than that. I was a helpless infant in a mental asylum.

I exchanged that book for a children's story, and took it back to my room where I sat on the edge of my bed and tried to read it. I hoped that I would be able to understand this level of literature at least, but again the words were completely unintelligible. I was dismayed. My mind was no longer my own. I was the most ignorant, useless nineteen-year-old in the world.

Someone had once told me that I was a born reader. I must have been proud of the praise because it stuck in my mind. Maybe I was a new person now – but perhaps I could find a way back to the person I used to be, relearn the skill that meant so much to me. I had no choice, so somehow I found the strength to persevere. I returned to the book again and again, determined to make sense of it. Eventually I made progress, finding that if I stayed calm and concentrated, I could piece some of the smaller words together.

From there I built up my stamina and my

understanding slowly returned. I never told anyone that I had a problem with reading. It was something I was ashamed of, it felt like evidence of my madness, so I battled it alone. It never occurred to me that if I'd confided in a member of the medical staff they might have been able to explain what had happened to me and why. It might have been a side effect of the medication or a phenomenon connected with my illness, a symptom that other patients shared, but I was convinced that I had to keep my 'weakness' a secret, to suffer in silence. I never told a soul about it, not even my family when they visited.

I had another upsetting and embarrassing problem. I often needed to pee urgently, but when I got to the toilet I couldn't go, although I was full to bursting. It was very painful and I used to sit on the toilet for what seemed like hours, in tears, but again the thought of confiding in someone about this never entered my head. I also developed an extremely acute sense of smell, which I found confusing. In an environment where a lot of people were unwashed and frightened it felt like an assault on my senses. I thought it must be yet more proof that my mind was mixed-up, that I was mad. Upset and disorientated, I added it to the growing list of things I was ashamed of, things I had to keep to myself.

My mother always said I was stubborn, and this trait proved useful when it came to teaching myself to read again. I practised daily to improve my concentration, determined not to lose the ability to read. When my mother visited, she insisted that I play table tennis with her or any other visitors who arrived while she was there, often one of my sisters. She made me keep score, telling me it was good for my concentration.

I found it hard to pin my mind down to the numbers, but I did as she said. I was a dutiful child.

I had no idea that my mother was drawing on her personal wisdom, and her nursing experience. I'd often heard others say that she was an excellent nurse, but I'd never seen any evidence of this. I knew her first as a submissive, passive wife, beaten down mentally by my over-bearing father then, after their divorce, sodden drunk every evening when she came home from work. But when I was ill in hospital and really needed her, she helped me more than anybody. And so quietly that I hardly noticed.

Hospitals are never restful places, but St Ann's was perhaps less peaceful than most. The room I slept in looked very much like an ordinary ward in a normal hospital. We had plastic jugs of water with plastic glasses on our plastic bedside cabinets. The blankets on the beds were thin and inadequate and the bay windows made loud cracking sounds all through the night. I never found out why this was – maybe it was the sound of tree branches knocking on them, or the UPVC contracting as the temperature fluctuated between day and night. Or, as I believed then, it could have been a plot by the nursing staff to keep all of us awake all night and therefore permanently insane.

One night, I had the most terrifying dream of my life. I couldn't remember all the details when I awoke. All I knew, and it was enough, was the vision I'd had of an enormous white horse carrying a man meant that I had witnessed the Apocalypse. I didn't know what that meant, or why I'd had the dream, and as usual I confided in no-one in case the information was used against me. I trusted nobody in that place.

Another night, something strange happened. This was not a dream or a trick of my imagination, it was a very real event. I was woken from what had been a deep sleep by two nurses, one of whom was holding a piece of paper and a pen. Together they insisted that I sign it, although they wouldn't let me see what the document was that I was putting my name to.

They were insistent, adamant that I sign it. A brainwave came to me from nowhere. I was sure it was a stroke of genius. Slowly and deliberately, I wrote 'Mickey Mouse' on the paper and handed it back. The nurses didn't notice what I had done, which disappointed me because I wanted recognition for my cleverness. I pointed it out to them and to my surprise they were furious and made me sign it again, using my real name.

I worried privately about that piece of paper for some time afterwards. My worst fear was that I had unintentionally agreed to have ECT, electro-convulsive therapy treatment, which was the thing I was most scared of in hospital. The drugs were bad enough, but the effects of those wore off. As I saw it, if I had ECT I would never be the same again, never be my true self. I'm not sure why this worried me so much, bearing in mind that I had never felt truly comfortable in my own skin. But I felt instinctively that ECT would destroy the core of me, whatever it was that made me an individual, and on no account did I want this to happen. Life might be painful, was often painful in my experience, but the thought of being permanently incapable of reasoned thought was unbearable. Perhaps I sensed that if that happened, I wouldn't remember all of this, and that I needed to. That one day I might be able to process the memories to help me work towards recovery, but only if

I could retrieve them. In any case, nothing became of the paper with my signature – or if it did, nobody told me about it.

I sat alone one afternoon, in the 'dormitory'. My visitors were due to arrive, but I needed a rest after my lunchtime dose of medication. I often walked off the morning dose. I would roam for miles if the ward door was left open. But I came back for lunch because I was ravenous. After lunch I regularly collapsed with exhaustion, not from the walking but because of the drugs. Anti-psychotic drugs are very strong tranquillisers.

On the cabinet by my bed were baskets of fruit and chocolates brought in for me by my family. I usually took no notice of them, but that afternoon I ate a small chocolate egg and then an apple. My sister Mandy came into the room with my mother and found me sitting on the edge of the bed, staring sadly into the bin on the floor. 'Look,' I said, pointing at the bin, at the apple core and the chocolate wrapper in it. 'The nurses are going to think I have a split personality because I have been eating chocolate and apples.' Everything, to me, was evidence of my madness, my inadequacy. I took no notice of my sister's reassurance, refusing to accept that any normal person could eat chocolate and then fruit.

The other patients who slept in the room were older than me and I was scared of most of them, although I never tried to get to know them. At least I wasn't alone, day or night. Although Mandy would repeatedly tell me that this place was a hospital, in the forefront of my mind was the knowledge that it was in fact a lunatic asylum, which meant that every person in it who was not a medical professional was a lunatic. I knew this instinctively because, whatever Mandy said, it looked and felt like nothing else. It was a grim and grisly, nightmare scenario of forced medication, deranged chain-smoking patients, constant fires in the long corridors and screaming suicidal people trying time and again to slit their arteries. I had never seen anything like it before and all I wanted was to get out.

When the ward door was closed and I couldn't go off walking, I occasionally sat in the television room with the other patients, all of us over-sedated and miserable. I joined in, if the nurses insisted, with whatever occupational therapy game they had devised. I found these embarrassing – not so long ago I had been at university, studying law; now I was a mental patient playing children's games. I couldn't see how this was going to aid my recovery.

One day in an occupational therapy session we were each given a slip of paper and asked to write down something that we would like to give another patient. My mind went completely blank. The others were writing things like 'a hug' or 'a kiss' but I shuddered at the thought of bodily contact with any of these people. They were ragged and dirty, smelling of body odour and cigarette smoke. We were told to stick our 'gift' onto the back of another patient, so I wrote 'money' and stuck it onto the back of a particularly impoverished-looking lady.

A young man called Tim, who was tall and wholesome-looking, but stooped in posture and oozing shyness from every pore, stuck his note onto my back. At the end of the game, when we were allowed to look, I saw that he had written 'Peace of mind'. 'Huh,' I thought cynically, 'He's obviously played this game before'.

I knew it was pointless to wish me peace of mind, in any case. Peace of mind would never be within my reach. My mind felt as if it was on fire for all my waking hours. Tight knots of confusion and panic were always present under the blanket of drugs I was forced to ingest. The only peace of mind I ever experienced was when I was asleep, and even then it wasn't complete. I had been plagued by sleep disturbances, dreams and nightmares, ever since I was a child. Peace of mind was a nice idea, but it had no basis in reality.

I blundered on through the days, doing my best to avoid occupational therapy. I roamed whenever I was able, as far and wide as I could manage. My legs were restless; they needed to keep moving and I had no choice except to follow. I walked endless circuits of the hospital grounds, or to the nearby beach. I gradually became aware that the terms of my section dictated that I should stay in the hospital grounds and that I wasn't supposed to wander any further. But the nurses were used to my disappearances and reappearances and either didn't notice or didn't care unless a visitor arrived, when they panicked over my whereabouts, which caused trouble.

I might have been allowed more freedom, but I was far from better. As a young child I was still, quiet and silent and as an adolescent I hardly spoke. But, in the hospital, I was reborn into a new, stupid version of my old self. I behaved like a remarkably dim, blundering child, wandering around the place drawing attention to myself, causing a nuisance.

I sat in the hospital foyer for hours, smoking, pestering strangers as they entered. I made a beeline for the lady who visited to take the patients' blood-samples for analysis. I imagined she was a vampire. The box she carried was marked in large letters PHLEBOTOMY, but to my deluded fancy it was clearly stamped TRANSYLVANIA. I was terrified of her, but determined that she shouldn't realise this, so I made a point of speaking to her as she arrived in the reception area. She soon learned to give me a wide berth, keeping her head down if she happened to see me as she walked into the hospital.

I didn't have much to do and often hung around the vending machines, spending the small change given to me by my sisters and mother. I filled up on junk food because the medication made me hungry and also because, out of the blue, I had decided to give up smoking and needed some other habit to take its place.

With hindsight, I think this was a sign that I was emerging from my troubled state. I had managed to work out that the cigarettes perpetually between my fingers were not a comfort after all, but a flag that signalled danger. A sign of madness. A clear marker of the difference between 'Us' and 'Them'. I decided to reject smoking as a quick and easy way to differentiate myself from all the crazy people. Mandy told me not to bother, that I had enough on my plate and should think about giving up smoking later, when I was better. But I sensed instinctively that I had no time to waste, and somehow, against the odds, found the strength to kick the habit.

5

A Voluntary Patient

I had a strong sense that the medical staff regarded me as a childish nuisance, wandering aimlessly around the hospital, as well as a potential hazard. This was all very new to me. I was used to being ignored, because as a child and young person I was an invisible presence, as meek and mild as anyone could have been. When I read Othello at school, I'd identified strongly with Desdemona, shy and blushing, scared of her own shadow.

But now everything had changed. I had an illness that had transformed my personality, and so I had been reclassified as posing a danger to myself or others. This was why I was being held under a section of the Mental Health Act, despite the fact that I had never attempted to hurt myself or anyone else. It was official, legal. I was unhinged, detached from myself and so the potential for damage and destruction was there. I had no choice but to believe all this about myself, although at a deeper level it didn't make much sense to me.

Time passed, and it didn't seem as if I was making much progress. It felt as if every day was like the one before it, and that nothing ever happened. I was wrong about this. The days were changing in form and shape, getting longer, brighter and warmer. In the physical world beyond the mental hospital, sunshine was breaking through.

I headed to the beach more often and stayed there longer each time. Nobody ever came looking for me, and I thought it was because they had realised I always came back at mealtimes. It was as if I was perpetually on the edge of starvation and although I hated the dining room, with its rows of metal dishes and unsmiling staff serving strange combinations of food, I was too hungry to resist the pull of the place.

What I hadn't realised was that technically I was free to leave. The 28-day section I'd legally been held under had expired, which meant I was now in the hospital as a voluntary patient. If I'd known this I'd have left the place like a shot, although I don't know where I would have gone. If I had asked any member of my family for shelter they would have insisted I return to the hospital, and I had nowhere else to stay.

It was immaterial anyway; I was unaware of my liberty and so I stayed put. Meanwhile, it wasn't just the outside world that was getting sunnier; light was gradually beginning to dawn in my mind. In the early days of my incarceration, I'd been convinced that the hospital menus were either intelligence tests or coded messages. When I chose Raspberry Fool for pudding, in my confused mind I was the Fool. When I chose Lamb Navarine as a main meal I was the Lamb of God who was being sacrificed. By selecting these options, I thought I was showing that I didn't care what 'they' thought. This backfired on me, because we were given our menus two days in advance, like a 'proper' hospital, so by the time the meals arrived I would have no memory of ordering whatever random thing I'd decided on and would believe that everyone was laughing at me. It was all rather troubling.

Now that I'd improved a little, I started to make better choices, depending on what I wanted to eat, and enjoyed the food more. I'd looked after myself from the start, washing as soon as I was permitted to, but now tasks like putting in my contact lenses each morning became easier. In the early days, my eyelids had been

33

made so heavy by the onslaught of medication that I'd have given up the fight and worn glasses instead, if my vanity had allowed it.

I was now allowed to have a bath whenever I wanted, and to my great relief nobody watched me do it. I washed my hair each day and brushed it out, letting it dry naturally. It was long, waist length, with light waves from a perm that had half-grown out. I chose my clothes carefully, spent ages fiddling with my make-up and putting concealer on my spots, and even made an effort to change my earrings regularly. It would have made more sense to let all this slide, but I was never one to let myself relax. Relaxation was not a word that had any part in my vocabulary.

I was told that I was recovering, and there were signs that this was the case. I still had plenty of visitors, unlike most of the other patients, and my mother in particular came most days. She never said much and we would sit together in silence unless I tried to entertain her with one of my meandering monologues, which she tended to disregard.

I knew my mother was upset to see me in this condition but I didn't know how to offer her any comfort. I loved her a lot and I felt very sorry for her, but I'd also started to harbour some resentment, wishing that she had shown interest in me and paid me some attention when I was younger. If only she had tried to connect with me, I thought, offered me some advice, I might not have found myself in this predicament. I often felt confused and alone, even when my mother was with me.

My sister Jane and her husband came to visit one day, with their baby. I loved Tom, and he was as beautiful as I remembered, bigger than when I had last seen him, his blue eyes shining brighter. He loved me too and laughed with delight to see me again. He held out his chubby finger, remembering the game we used to play. I touched it with the end of my finger, saying 'ZZZZ!', pretending I was giving him an electric shock, knowing this would make him laugh.

But as we touched, I felt Tom's baby mind taking over mine, garnering all the knowledge within it, leaving my brain as empty as a cloudless sky. I could see all my thoughts in the crafty, blue eyes of the baby who had stolen them.

My friends from university visited, one by one, but none of them ever returned. Why would they? I was an alien, a freak. When I saw them I wondered vaguely how they had found me, although on another level I knew it was my own doing. I often fed the pay phone at the end of the ward endless streams of 10p and 20p pieces, calling in favours from everyone I had ever known, asking them to come and visit, to rescue me.

I looked forward to visitors, but when they arrived I was upset, embarrassed by my surroundings and the depths to which I had fallen and I often became incoherent and rambling. I seemed to fall in and out of madness, and although the periods of lucidity were happening more frequently I still didn't have much control over myself.

I escaped into the recesses of my mind to avoid the shame I felt, and then became a blithering idiot, which upset and worried my guests. No wonder they never made repeat appearances. But my family still visited. I was happy to see them, whatever my state of mind, although I didn't like it when Mandy brought her boyfriend along one day. This was a part of my life I would have preferred to keep private, if only I could.

One day I was wandering around the ward, distracted, and a young nurse stopped me and asked how I felt. I replied with a stream of nonsense but she interrupted me. 'No,' she insisted. 'How do you feel?'

'I have a headache,' I told her, surprising myself with this information. She gave me paracetamol, and for a while the din in my head receded.

6
Medication

By now I had been on a cocktail of pills for months. I was prescribed a variety of anti-psychotic drugs. These used to be known as major tranquillisers but had been re-branded. I deeply resented what seemed to me to be a brutal regime of medication, which made me feel as though I'd been subjected to a chemical cosh.

The main drug was chlorpromazine, also called Largactil, which came in liquid or tablet form. The liquid tasted foul and I worried about the possibility of it hurting my mouth or my throat. I was told that the progression to tablets happened when the nurses could be sure that I wasn't trying to hide the tablet under my tongue or palm it (like hurting myself in the bath, this had not occurred to me as a possibility until they mentioned it).

When I was finally given the tablets instead, they still worried me, because they were stamped with the letters LG. I thought the tablets had been marked with my initials and this must be due to some kind of a sinister plot, although the nurses insisted that it was the pharmacy code for Largactil.

I would wander around the hospital with my fists clenched tight at my sides, and the nurses laughed and joked about getting me a punch-bag. My mother, who was usually very placid, became annoyed because she recognised the condition of my hands as a side effect of one of the drugs. She insisted that the nursing staff should find a way to remedy the tension and rigidity in my muscles and so a magic pill, procyclidine, was prescribed. This worked against the side effects of the other drugs, relaxing my muscles and allowing my fists to unclench. I was now taking four or five tablets three times a day, but at least I was physically more comfortable.

My behaviour was still very unsettled. I couldn't sleep at night so I stayed up, trying to talk to whichever nurse was on duty, asking them pointless questions, challenging their authority like an annoying adolescent.

It took a few weeks before the night staff found a way to silence me; I was prescribed sleeping pills, which I thought were a godsend. At last, I was able to rest and recuperate, at least during the night hours. I much preferred these drugs to the daytime ones.

On a table by the door of the room where I slept, I kept a pile of loose-leaved paper that I called my 'Book'. I had written these disturbed outpourings when I was becoming ill, during my stay at Jane and Tony's flat. I claimed it was the story of my life, but really it was pure lunacy spilling across the pages. I wasn't sure how the 'Book' had followed me to the hospital but I continued to write in it regularly, although it became more of a journal than an attempt at a narrative.

I left the 'Book' in public view deliberately, but I was shocked one morning when I arrived back on the ward from my wanderings to find a cluster of men in suits huddled around the pile of papers, reading. They dispersed when I arrived. I still have no idea who they might have been; a team of visiting doctors, or outriders from the Mental Health Tribunal, perhaps? I was suddenly convulsed with shame that I had left the innermost workings of my troubled mind out on display. I shredded the 'Book' into tiny fragments, destroying the evidence of my diseased soul.

I gave up any hopes of a literary career around

that time. I associated this dream with the memory of my attempted escape when I was first sectioned, running hell-for-leather from the hospital in my nightwear shouting, 'I am a writer!' I burned with embarrassment whenever I remembered this, and decided that from then on I would deny this ghastly apparition, the part of myself that held ridiculous notions and harboured delusions of grandeur.

Writing was the raft that I had clung to when I felt myself slipping into madness, and now I was starting to heal, I discarded it. The combination of strong tranquillisers and bodily exhaustion had finally calmed me and made me into something approaching my former, quiet self.

As my health improved, the stream of visitors abated. I was able to hold a conversation, and my weekly meetings with Dr Patel lasted a little longer. He was interested to know whether I had been sexually abused in childhood. I felt that it would have been to my benefit to say I had, because it would have provided some excuse for my breakdown, which had caused me such shame and embarrassment. I was a truthful person, though. I had a strong sense of morality, gained, I think, from the many books I had read as a child; more than my share of Enid Blyton, but also plenty of classical authors. I'd gained a real education from these stories, which provided an anchor throughout my chaotic and confusing childhood years. I'd learned the difference between right and wrong from my books and I put great value on it.

So, although I felt some pressure to say yes, feeling that everyone around me would be relieved to have an explanation for my mental breakdown, I couldn't act dishonourably. I told the truth. I had not been sexually abused. I had not really been physically abused at all. My father might have slapped me occasionally, but it was never painful; the distress I had suffered had all been emotional. My father's torrents of verbal abuse, foul accusations, swearing, had struck terror into my heart, but it did not, I felt, explain why I had ended up in St Ann's.

It was understandable that the doctor questioned whether I'd been sexually abused, because I had exhibited some bizarre sexual behaviour. My mind had started to unravel at the end of the spring term at university. I had a boyfriend but I developed a crush on one of my fellow students and basically stalked the poor chap, although he had tried to make it clear that he wasn't interested. I then found another boyfriend, closer to home. And then in the hospital itself I formed a relationship with a patient who was a lot older than me and had already been in and out of St Ann's for years. I was a mess, an embarrassing disaster, and all my troubles, I felt, were entirely of my own making. There was no hope for me.

7
Scott

As I became more coherent, a young doctor developed an interest in my case and asked if I would meet him for weekly consultations. I can't remember his surname, but his first name was Scott (my mother's name was also Scott, which I considered to be a remarkable coincidence. My mind was wired to make connections between random occurrences.)

Scott was young, tall, American, impossibly good-looking. He had blond hair, was self-assured and tanned. I had never set eyes on a more attractive man, and I was smitten. I was also embarrassed by his attention and would have avoided the meetings if I'd felt able, but he was a doctor; I bowed to his authority.

We met once a week in a large room with a conference table, just the two of us. I answered his questions briefly and reluctantly, suspicious of his interest. One day when I refused to speak to him at all, he seemed hurt. 'I thought we were friends,' he said.

I was sure he must be laughing at me. How could a person like him want to be friends with a person like me? What was there to like about me, especially in this situation? I refused to trust him or open up, but he continued to probe into my life, and one day I told him about my mother's alcoholism. It was never spoken about at home and I felt I was breaking a huge taboo by confiding in the doctor.

His response terrified me. 'Don't you think it's dangerous,' he asked, 'that she has a responsible job at the hospital and such a bad drinking problem?' I had never considered how my mother's alcoholism might affect her work and I didn't want to think about it now. I was petrified that because I had betrayed her confidence, my mother would lose her job, fall deeper into the abyss and drink herself to death. And this would all be my fault.

I begged Scott not to tell anyone and he promised he wouldn't, but I didn't believe him. I was inconsolable. I had another couple of meetings with him after that, but I never opened up again, staying silent or speaking in monosyllables. He must have realised eventually that he wasn't going to get anywhere and our meetings tailed off.

When I was out on one of my meanders through the nearby village I often saw Scott's athletic figure jogging along alone, disciplined, keeping himself fit and strong. He smiled and waved when he passed me. I would smile back weakly, feeling sick at the thought of how pathetic I was compared to him, how ludicrous his suggestion of friendship. I never believed that I was worth a minute of his time and attention.

8
Characters

There were other characters in what I thought of as a performance, a show of madness. Some lines from Macbeth often flitted through my mind; 'Life's but a walking shadow, a poor player/That struts and frets his hour upon the stage/And then is heard no more. It is a tale/Told by an idiot, full of sound and fury/Signifying nothing.'

I related to all of that. Maybe it was because what happened in the hospital seemed so unreal, so unnecessarily dramatic, or because the way I felt about things could change so rapidly, but I did feel at times that I was a character in a play.

A lot of the young men and women in St Ann's were addicted to drugs and were undergoing rehab treatment. They were kept in a separate ward and I sensed that they looked down on the rest of us, who had no real excuse for our 'madness'.

It was hard to differentiate between the two groups. There was a massive chap I thought of as Erik the Viking, who was tall and wide, with long, flaming-red hair. He caused a lot of trouble, raging and shouting around the hospital, setting off the fire alarms by starting fires in the tall, metal ashtrays that were situated everywhere.

I never learned Eric the Viking's real name, but often passed him on my way to the village or the beach. Whenever I did, he would smile kindly at me, and tell me, 'Always walk on the sunny side of the street.' I appreciated the sentiment, although I did tend to worry about sunburn.

I was very upset the day I saw Erik flat out on

the floor of the day room, surrounded by nurses. He'd managed to slice through both of his wrists. There was an awful lot of blood.

Alan was in his early twenties, handsome, charming. He claimed to have been the victim of a serious car crash and said he'd had a personality change as a consequence, although I wondered why he didn't carry any physical scars. I didn't see any sign of the personality change either, for some time. He seemed to be completely rational in fact, until the day I was leaving the lounge and glanced back to see him calmly showing off his penis to another male patient.

Another chap, Steve, looked odd; he was short, with long hair and large, protruding ears and he behaved in a very peculiar way, spending most of his day walking around and around the table tennis table, talking to himself. One day, he sat down at the piano and, with no sheet music, played a concerto like a maestro, although the piece ended in a crashing crescendo of pure dissonance. Just one more thing for me to ponder over.

I still tried to avoid the television lounge. I'd had a fixation on electricity since my breakdown started and I still wasn't sure whether I could trust it. While I was staying with Jane, when I was first becoming mad, I seemed to be crackling with electricity. Anybody who touched me got an electric shock, and I'd get some very bad shocks myself, particularly when I was getting into or out of my car.

At St Ann's, the TV screen seemed to move and flicker when I entered the room, as if I was causing some sort of electrical interference. It worried me. I wanted to watch TV more as I got better and became able to concentrate for longer, and I noticed that the screen was gradually becoming more stable when I was around. I was still obsessed with the flickering though and I watched the screen itself more than the programmes. When my mother visited, I asked her why the picture was so unclear and she told me she hadn't really noticed, but perhaps the area had bad reception or the aerial might be at fault. I still thought it was something to do with me.

One day I was hovering at the door to the TV lounge and one of the patients called out, 'Come in Louise, and calm the television down!' This alarmed and confused me, because I believed I was the only person who had noticed the effect I had on the screen. I didn't reply, but quickly turned and left.

After a while I realised that we patients shared some common delusions or experiences, which was strange in itself because the delusions were so bizarre. One day when I was newly arrived on Sandbanks Ward, for example, I went barefoot to the bathroom to have a wash, carrying my flannel and toothbrush.

As I walked, I felt something sticky under my feet and looked down to see that I had trodden in what looked like toothpaste. What frightened me was that instead of leaving footprints in this substance, I had left pawprints. I was appalled and also, for some reason, ashamed. When I looked around I saw a group of elderly patients watching me, and I realised they were laughing at me.

Another day, I met a young man in the occupational therapy room, who was visibly anxious. He was busy writing, and when I asked to see what he'd written he refused, saying that I'd find it too upsetting. Eventually he agreed to show me, and he'd written an account in which he was walking along, looked behind him, and saw the Devil's pawprints.

I was struck by the fact that we'd both had a similar experience. I couldn't help feeling a little suspicious too. Were the other patients or the nursing staff playing tricks on us? But why would anybody do such a thing?

Many years later, I discovered that, strange as they are, the symptoms of psychosis (the term for a serious disturbance of the thoughts) have remained remarkably similar over time. For example, in the twentieth century, people in the throes of a breakdown might have thought they were being personally addressed by the television or the radio, as happened to me. A hundred years ago, before broadcasting, people might believe that the preacher in church or on a soapbox in the street was talking only to them. I wish I'd known, as a terrified nineteen-year-old in St Ann's, that I was not alone, that thousands of people had suffered in similar ways over the centuries, and that many of them had recovered completely.

It was in the occupational therapy room at St Ann's that I discovered I had completely lost my sense of humour. One of the staff showed me a mug emblazoned with a joke and said, 'This will make you laugh.' I gazed at it for ages, trying to work out how it could be amusing, but I couldn't get it.

When I couldn't read I had felt lost but this was different, perhaps because I had never found life very funny to begin with. Laughter I could live without, but literature I could not.

Most of the women in the ward were older than me. Susan stood at the end of the ward near the call box, as if she was permanently on guard. She frequently waylaid me, telling me how her daughter had been raped by a relative and she had been powerless to help. I never saw any daughter but I believed Susan's story because it was etched in the deep, dark semi-circles under her eyes. I found it distressing and would have avoided her if I could. I made up my mind that Susan must be an angel, and I told her so every time I passed by. 'I wish I was,' she always replied sadly.

One girl, Helen, was even younger than me, just fifteen. She told me her mother had sent her to the hospital because she couldn't look after her at home. Helen accepted this calmly, but I was indignant on her behalf. She was always laughing and joking and telling me everything about her state of mind, although I wished she wouldn't. I liked her a lot and had no idea why her mother might have found her difficult to cope with, other than the fact that she never stopped talking.

I wouldn't have admitted it, even to myself, but the madness, the falling away, could sometimes be fun. I remember Helen and I giggling away like schoolgirls when we were having our nails manicured by volunteers from the Red Cross, although I have no idea what we found so funny.

Sally was in her early twenties. She was an addict and she didn't seem to mind being in the hospital at all. She spent most of her time curled up on the window seat in the day room like a cat, surveying the room through half-closed eyes. She seemed to have given in completely to the tranquillising effects of the psychiatric medication. Perhaps, to her, they were just free drugs.

Sally made me wonder whether perhaps I should

just capitulate too. But I couldn't stand being controlled, and so I fought the effects of the drugs. My medication was gradually reduced, until I was taking only one tablet of chlorpromazine, or Largactil, three times a day, with procyclidine at lunch time and a sleeping tablet every night. The power of these was astonishing. The moment I swallowed one I fell instantly into a deep, dreamless sleep until the next morning.

I welcomed the enforced rest, in a way, but I still resented the tranquillising effects of the daytime medication. I started to skip the lunchtime tablets and nobody seemed to notice or care, I guess because the Mental Health Act section under which I was held had expired, although I still had no idea of this. I noticed that I felt very panicky when I skipped a dose, and this scared me. I started to worry that I wouldn't manage without them so, more often than not, I queued up and took them obediently.

I had become 'compliant' but I still hated St Ann's and everything it stood for. Some of the nurses, I knew, were decent people. Others were not. As I recovered, I started to wonder why they were allowed to work there. The good nurses didn't judge me, didn't intervene unless I asked them for help or advice. They were caring and compassionate. They inspired a desire to recover, to join the outside world again. The bad nurses made their patients lose all faith in humanity and all desire to be part of it.

Although I could distinguish between the quality of the nursing staff and no longer considered them all to be evil, I couldn't see anything positive about the treatment I had received in St Ann's. One day, the staff told me I was better, and it was time for me to be discharged from the hospital. However, they added, I would have to continue taking the medication as a prophylactic measure long into the future, perhaps for ever, to make sure I didn't get ill again.

Taking long-term psychiatric medication to prevent future illness didn't really make sense to me. I didn't object though, partly because I knew that I wasn't better at all, in the sense of being free of emotional distress. I was no longer incoherent, but I still felt perpetually anxious, edgy and ill at ease. I didn't admit to this, though, in case the date set for my discharge should be delayed.

St Ann's was a lovely Victorian mansion in Canford Cliffs, one of the most exclusive areas of Dorset. But the months I spent there had been the most dismal experience of my life, and all I wanted was to get as far away from the place as I possibly could. When I finally left, on 4 July 1988, I was determined that I would never return.

9
Back to the Beginning

St Ann's had been the worst of times, but my life had never been a bed of roses. My earliest memories, which are now a hazy jumble, are rooted in a large country house, Harrow Lodge, the former hotel in Hampshire where we lived from 1969, when I was just a year old. Before that, my family lived somewhere in the north of England, which I thought of as a distant, foreign country.

The top of the long, gravel driveway that swept to our home still bore the sign, 'Harrow Lodge Hotel'. The house was a wonderful place. It had a library, well-supplied with beautifully bound volumes, a ballroom and a bar, still stocked with glasses and drinks left over from the days before we moved in. There were countless bedrooms, bathrooms, storerooms and spaces that nobody used except for us children, crammed with items that nobody else knew existed.

My parents' suite of rooms was spectacular. The bedroom had long, heavy curtains that opened using an electric foot pedal, and their en-suite bathroom featured a bidet and an enormous corner bath with gold-plated taps.

I was proud of this evidence of our family's wealth and I was also proud that we were a big family. My father had nine children, four with my mother and the others with his two previous wives. He had gained full custody of all his children after both of his divorces but some of my older siblings had left home before I was born, and others were away at school. Jane, Stephen and I were the youngest and we banded together.

There was a lot to do at Harrow Lodge, for a trio of mischievous pre-schoolers. We made the most of the huge, mostly empty house and grounds. We slid three flights down the back staircase on mattresses, dragged them up to the attic and slid down again. There was a whole room filled with sheets, blankets and pillows from the old hotel and we used these to make camps in the acres of overgrown thickets that encircled the house. It didn't matter when they perished over time, we just made new ones.

As the eldest and most active of the three of us, Jane cooked up endless creative plans for play. There were unused outbuildings that we made into clubhouses, summer houses to play in, orchards to rifle through. We cut the bamboo that had grown tall around the edges of the lawns and made bows and arrows out of it, practising archery for hours on end.

Jane and I had our own dogs, Jack Russell terriers. Jane's was called Scrapper, a feisty little wiry-coated creature, black with a few white spots. My dog, Buster, was his opposite, smoother-coated and milder-mannered, white with a few black patches.

I adored Buster, but he was also a source of secret shame. When I was alone with him in my bedroom, I pretended to be angry with him, shouted at him loudly for no reason at all and then ignored him. When I then changed tack and began to be kind again, the poor dog would be grateful and make a huge fuss of me in return. I felt bad for behaving like this, but something compelled me to repeat the cruel game again and again.

I loved Harrow Lodge, with its numerous symmetrical windows facing carefully tended lawns. I often stood on our front lawn, looking back at the whole vista picking out my bedroom from the range of windows, fifth from the left in the middle of a section of three, Jane's room to one side and Stephen's to the other.

There was a large open-fronted summerhouse with sturdy brick walls, where I liked to sit and read when I was left to my own devices. I read Enid Blyton of course, and all the Just William books. I read books of Greek and Latin myths and visualised King Midas at the well nearby, growing the ears of an ass because he shouted his secret into the depths when he should have known better, should have kept his big mouth shut.

Beyond the lawn was a large field. My elder sisters used to keep their ponies there, but when they left for boarding school the ponies vanished, the grass grew long and the field was let to the farmer in the next house along the lane. Once a year he made the grass into hay and the three of us, thick as thieves, climbed and tumbled in the haystacks.

Our parents were often away in my early years, and a succession of nannies looked after the three of us. I liked all these girls, but I loved one of them, Sue Balogh, and I believed she loved me too. On my birthday Sue gave me a soft toy, a Kanga with a small Roo in its pouch. Jane seethed with jealousy, not of the toy, but of the special connection I shared with the nanny. Jane liked people to prefer her to me, and they usually did, because she was a lot more fun.

The nannies tended not to stick around for long, and we usually didn't know where they had gone, or why. Sue left one day too, and after that there were no more nannies, only the three of us, aged three, four and five, free to roam the grounds of Harrow Lodge.

We lost ourselves in play, pretending to be Red

Indians, or policemen. One day Jane and I, dressed as squaws, tied our little brother, hands behind his back, to a tree. We wandered off, got distracted, and came back later than we meant to, to find Stephen miserable and crying, his wrists rubbed red-raw.

My father was rarely at home when I was very young. When he was there, he liked to boast to visitors about how early I'd learned to read. He tried to show off my skills, asking me to spell out long words to them. I hated this. I knew I wasn't as brilliant as he thought I was, and I often got the spellings wrong and embarrassed us both.

Dad was sixteen years older than Mum, and they were a world apart to look at. He was overweight and out of shape. He always wore a full three-piece suit, shirt and tie; she was slim, elegant and beautifully dressed in the latest fashions. It was a puzzle.

I knew that my father was a businessman or, in his own words, 'a self-made millionaire', but I didn't know what his money-making empire consisted of. I did know that he was often away from home and so was my mum. This changed over time. He began to be at home more frequently, and his temper became increasingly frayed. He often exploded, shouting and swearing at us for various childish offences. When this happened, we'd run off and hide outside until we judged that he had calmed down and we could risk going back into the house.

I often daydreamed, imagining that I had been adopted and my real parents would eventually arrive to rescue me. One day, I read the story of the Princess and the Pea, about a little girl who couldn't sleep at night. Mattresses were piled on her bed one after another, to make it softer, but it didn't help. It was only when a tiny pea was discovered under the bottom mattress that everybody realised she must be a princess as nobody else could have been so sensitive. She was duly whisked off to her rightful home.

I decided to try this for myself. I hid a pea under my mattress, and then began to drop heavy hints to Jean, our housekeeper, about how I couldn't sleep at night. She took no notice and eventually I led her to the mattress and 'discovered the pea' for her. She was annoyed, telling me what a silly girl I was, and missing the point entirely. She was right, I was a silly girl. Also, I had used a cooked pea instead of a dried one, and the result was a flat, squidged mess.

I didn't really want to be rescued. I would have missed my mother too much. I adored her, and wished that I saw her more often. She was gentle and kind, an oasis of calm in the confusing world of Harrow Lodge. She was clever, too. Whenever I asked her the meaning of a word in whatever book I was reading, she knew the answer.

Now that my parents were largely at home, Mum bathed Jane, Stephen and I together, singing to us sweetly throughout the process. She picked the peeling paint off the steamy bathroom walls with her fingernails to sculpt images of Disney characters, Bambi and the Little Mermaids. She was a marvel, and when she was with us she made everything right.

An undercurrent of unease ran through the house. My father's bouts of anger became more intense and more frequent. Stress was building, like a geyser waiting to burst, although we three kids had no idea why. We tried to avoid it, escaping into our glorious outdoor playground, climbing trees, sheltering in the bamboo thickets. We watched the Lone Ranger on TV, tried to enact it in our private Wild West.

Sometimes we hung out with Grandma, our father's mother, who lived with us. Grandma was Jewish, which meant that we were partly Jewish too. Her parents had escaped from Russia. She was one of many children, although we never met any of her siblings. Grandma had her own sitting room, in the bar next to the ballroom. She sat there all day watching television, immaculately dressed in gold-threaded skirt suits, garnished with shimmering brooches. She told us that her special, precious little boy had bought her these lovely things. Mum told us to be kind to her, because she had senile dementia, so we never corrected her, although we knew that it was really our huge, old, angry father who gave them to her.

We loved Grandma but we were wild children, and we often amused ourselves by hiding behind the armchairs in her sitting room and jumping out to scare her. She never minded. After she'd recovered from the shock, she would reach in her handbag for the ever-present paper bag of sweets and offer them around. She was kind and she was very good at sharing, and it didn't matter a bit that she didn't understand us at all, or we her.

As I got older, I listened closely to my father and tried to work out what he did for a living, but it never became clear. He boasted of owning bingo halls and said he had a licence to print money. That sounded good. We needed protection, according to my father, so we kept dogs at Harrow Lodge, not only Buster and Scrapper, but Alsations, lots of them. They were pets as well as guard dogs.

I remember my dad sitting like a lord in his favourite armchair, chain-smoking and talking on the phone. He smoked as if the cigarette was part of him. Sometimes he became lost in thought and forgot he was holding one. When this happened, we kids sat at his feet, watching in awe as the ash grew longer and longer, like an impossible horizontal tower burning up towards his nicotine-stained fingers. He was immobile and oblivious, then he'd remember himself and flick the ash into one of the glass or onyx ashtrays. Then he'd take a puff, hold his breath for a moment and blow the smoke straight out into the room. At other times he didn't see the ash building at all and it would reach the point where we had to call out to alert him to the impending disaster. 'Ash, Dad, ash! Ash! ASH!' Startled from his reverie, he would shift his bulk in the chair, but the sudden movement usually only toppled the tower of ash onto the floor, the chair or his suit. He would look down at us, smile vaguely and brush the ash away. Stub the cigarette into the ashtray. Light another to replace it.

Dad told us that he'd started smoking when he was seven and had been sent to board at Brighton College. He'd hated it, talked about the terror he'd felt when he was left there, and how he had been bullied. When he spoke that way, I wondered why, in that case, he'd sent Mandy and Belita to Roedean School, which was also in Brighton, and whether they were happy.

I never questioned my father about his childhood years. I wish I'd known more, so I could have understood him better, but nobody ever dared questioned my father about anything. His rages were violent and dangerous, and we lived in fear of provoking one. After he'd calmed down from a fit of temper, he'd say that he'd been 'in a diabetic state', which was his attempt at an apology. His diabetes had started suddenly and my mother (who had trained as a nurse when she was young) had been instructed by the doctor in how to inject him with insulin. He didn't like the injections, and after a while he decided he would only take tablets for his illness. They were littered around Harrow Lodge, vast containers of pills, some orange and others slate grey, all of them enormous. Horse pills, he called them.

Diabetes, I thought, was no excuse for bad behaviour.

10
No Smoke Without Fire

When I was very young, our family went on a lot of holidays. I remember flying with British Airways first class to Disney World. I remember getting badly sunburned, at a hotel in Florida. I remember flying to Portugal where James Callaghan, who later became the British Prime Minister, stayed in the same hotel as us. Although I don't remember it, my father often boasted that he and I got along very well.

One night in the Portuguese hotel, I was silently fuming underneath the dinner table. I can't remember why I'd been sent to eat my food under the table, but I did know that it was unfair. My family were all laughing at me, which I hated. It was my father's fault, everything always was, and I suddenly felt the injustice of it all. I knew what I had to do. I plunged my fork into his leg as hard as I could, and he shouted out in anger and shock, 'The fucking child fucking stabbed me!'

Time stood still. I braced myself for retaliation. My life was over, I knew it. But then to my amazement, my father began to laugh and everybody else around the table joined in. I'd got a reprieve, a pardon, but I was not happy, because this turn of events made no more sense than anything ever had in my world. Worse, it made me feel more powerless than usual. It must have been a relief to Jane not to have been punished for once. As the eldest of the three of us, she was usually blamed whenever we 'kids' did anything wrong.

It wasn't always Jane's fault, of course. She wasn't involved at all when Stephen and I carried out a series of experiments with fire that could have been fatal. He had got hold of a large box of matches, which wouldn't have been hard to do at Harrow Lodge – both of our parents smoked with a vengeance and there were ashtrays, matches and lighters all over the place.

I don't remember ever making a plan, or discussing what we were doing, but every morning for about a week Stephen woke me up quietly and the two of us crept downstairs and made a little fire in the conservatory, out of newspaper. When it started to spread, he stamped it out with his new, thick-soled shiny black shoes, and then we crept back to our rooms.

Nobody noticed the scorches on the conservatory carpet. Stephen and I didn't really think we were doing any harm, although we understood the need to keep our activities secret. As the days wore on, we became more daring and the fires grew larger. One morning one of the gardeners spotted us from outside, through the glass. Our latest fire was blazing merrily, and we could tell from his face that he was going to spill the beans.

We obviously needed to take action. Stephen used his special shoes to stamp out the blaze as usual, then we gathered up our newspapers and the matches and moved to our playroom at the end of the corridor. It was here that our father found us, giggling happily as our latest creation blazed merrily away in the centre of the room. That turned out to be our last fire.

It was unusual for Stephen to be the cause of any trouble. He was a lovely little boy, with long, blond curls and everyone doted on him. Jane and I treated him as our plaything, teasing him mercilessly. One day, we dressed him up in a set of flouncy white petticoats, for fun. But as we were standing back to admire our handiwork, our mother called up the stairs. 'Stephen? I need you, now. We have to go out to buy your school uniform.'

'He's not ready yet,' Jane shouted back. We struggled to hold back our giggles.

'I don't care,' yelled Mum. 'Send him downstairs, this minute.'

'She asked for it,' muttered Jane, forcing Stephen into his heavy overcoat. We buttoned it up together, then bustled him down the stairs to our mother. He trotted obediently after her, not saying a word.

Mum came home a few hours later. 'I was mortified,' she told us. 'I took my son's coat off in the middle of Marks and Spencer's to find him dressed in petticoats!'

Mum was cross, but we weren't scared of her like we were of our father. 'Why didn't you pretend he was a girl?' said Jane. 'He looks like one!' She took my hand and we ran off together, still giggling.

When I was seven, my father told me that he had seven million pounds and he was going to give his children a million pounds each when we were eighteen. I didn't believe him. Most of my elder siblings were already a lot older than eighteen and anyway he had nine children, not seven. He couldn't even do basic maths.

60

Nor did I believe him on the many occasions he promised to give me his personalised number plate (LG 1) when I was old enough to drive. I couldn't see the point of it anyway. I knew my own initials. I didn't need everybody else to know them.

On other occasions my father fell into racist rants, and at these times I kept very quiet. There was no point trying to contradict him, but I had many friends at boarding school by then who had different skin tones and I knew very well that this didn't matter at all.

In fact, the older I grew, the less I trusted my father and the more I believed that he was not a very good person. It made me sad, because I had loved him dearly when I was very small. But I reached the point that whenever my father said anything, I believed it was a safe bet that the opposite would be true.

I felt sorry for my mother, who seemed to take the brunt of his verbal abuse. He wasn't the sort to physically hurt people, but I was sure that whoever coined the phrase, 'Sticks and stones may break my bones, but words will never hurt me,' had not had the pleasure of meeting my father.

One day, something strange happened. I was alone, outside, at the back of the house and I caught sight of my reflection in one of the windows. I was about eight years old then, a serious child with shortish, straight hair. I was always dressed practically and plainly, usually in Jane's cast-off clothes.

But although the face that gazed back at me was my own, the child I saw had curly hair, cut and styled in a short bob. She wore a fancy, Victorian dress. I stared at her. I was uneasy and a little scared. How was it possible for someone to have my face but old-fashioned hair and clothes? The child stared back impassively until I turned tail and ran away.

It was around the same time that I became aware that my father's business, whatever it was, was failing. He talked about putting in a bid for the Swan Hunter shipyard, but nothing became of it. He stopped speaking about bingo halls, and never mentioned his 'licence to print money' again. Then he set up a business, the confusingly titled 'Victorian Paintings Limited', which sold jewellery from the huge dining room at Harrow Lodge.

We children were employed as unpaid assistants in this makeshift shop, at weekends and in the school holidays. We had to help load the glass cabinets with jewellery every morning and unload them every evening. It was a heavy and thankless task, but we carried it out without complaint.

In 1977 my mother's mother, our Granny, died. Mum was beside herself with grief. She wandered up and down the corridors of the house, crying. My father hated to see her like this, but he didn't try to comfort her. Instead, he bullied, harangued and swore at her in frustration until she gradually returned, over a few days, to her former quiet, submissive self.

The same year, our Grandma died. The sitting room where she once sat was now empty. It was the end of an era. We children all felt the loss of her presence, and in my case it was tinged with guilt, knowing how we had taken her for granted, teased her sometimes. Of course, my father must have suffered deeply over the loss of his mother, as my mother had done when Granny had passed away, but I don't remember being aware of it at the time.

11
Durlston Court

School and home were two distinct worlds. My first school was Durlston Court, in Barton-on-Sea, Hampshire. It was a private preparatory school, which educated children from the age of four to thirteen. The idea was that at thirteen, the children would take the 'Common Entrance' exam for public school.

Since I had an October birthday, I was nearly five when I started at Durlston Court. Jane was only sixteen months older than me, but she had a June birthday and so was two school years ahead. I was not good at making friends, so I was lost and lonely at school and often trailed around behind Jane and her friends in the playground, but she was happy and popular and usually too busy to notice me.

I was not only lonely, I was also bored. Nothing about school made any sense to me. We were expected to sit at our desks for hours, reading books with three or four very large words on each page. I found it baffling.

One morning I sat, sullenly looking at the Peter and Jane book I had been given. I had already flicked through it and found nothing of interest. The teacher came over to scold me, 'Come on, Louise. Read the book.'

'I have read it,' I told her.

She was cross. 'No, I mean read the words. Don't just look at the pictures.'

'I have read it,' I repeated. Did this woman not understand English?

She picked up another book from a nearby shelf. 'Right then,' she said briskly. 'Let's hear you read this one. Aloud.'

The new book had about twenty words on each page but was still a long way from interesting. 'Peter and Jane had a dog,' I read rapidly. 'The dog had a ball. Peter threw the ball. The ball went over the fence. The dog got the ball...'

I looked up and my voice trailed off. The teacher was staring at me in silence, and I couldn't read her expression. 'Right,' she said, and walked off.

I was terrified. I'd obviously done something wrong and was going to be in trouble. I hadn't yet seen any adults in the school shouting, swearing or chasing children around as my father did at home, but I was sure that this was about to happen.

A few minutes later the teacher returned, with the Headmistress, Miss Vyse. They towered above me, solemnly. 'Pick up your chair, Louise, and follow me,' said the Headmistress. Now I definitely knew what was going to happen. I had read about things like this in books. I was going to have to sit on my chair in the corridor, as a punishment. Well, that wasn't so bad.

But that wasn't what happened. Miss Vyse walked beside me and opened a door at the end of the corridor. 'This is your new class,' she said. I had been moved up a year group. The dozens of eyes goggling at me as I found a space for myself and my chair in the crowded room belonged to my new classmates.

Miss Vyse was my new teacher. She was very strict. We spent a large part of each day reading Peter and Jane books, which I found very dull. I had been used to reading proper stories, mostly Enid Blyton books, which allowed the imagination to soar. Peter and Jane, on the other hand, were the most boring children on the planet and spent most of their time playing in their small garden with a ball and a dog, doing nothing interesting at all. Jane and I had more fun in a day at Harrow Lodge, making wigwams and bows and arrows and teasing our younger brother, than Peter and Jane had in the whole of their boring lives with their stupid, boring dog.

I was very isolated. I found it hard to talk to anyone, so I still didn't make any friends. I only spoke when I had to, in class. When we weren't reading about stupid Peter and boring Jane, we sang nursery rhymes like 'Row the Boat' or coloured in pictures or played with wooden shapes. I had landed in some sort of a kindergarten.

I didn't do a lot of drawing or colouring, but I liked the wooden shapes. We got the chance to play with clay, which I enjoyed. And Miss Vyse taught us all the times tables. We had to chant them by rote every day, which at least was new and different.

When I was about seven years old, ready to move to the upper part of Durlston, I was told that I had been entered for an internal scholarship. An English teacher came down from the upper part of the school and introduced himself. 'I'm Andrew Ransome. I'll be carrying out the tests.'

There were three of us sitting the scholarship. We each had to write a story, then do a jigsaw puzzle while chatting to Mr Ransome. He was gentle and encouraging, expressing surprise when I told him I'd never seen a jigsaw before. When I got stuck, I cried out in frustration, 'I can't!'

He replied calmly, 'There's no such word as can't.'

'Well then,' I said grumpily, 'Can not.' He burst

out laughing, but not mockingly. I liked this man. He was laughing with me, not at me.

I did finish the jigsaw and won the scholarship, which meant a reduction in my school fees. My father liked to boast about it, and I felt a mixture of pride and embarrassment when he did this. It seemed that the only thing that mattered about me was my brains. I didn't have as much belief in my intellectual ability as my father did, and this worried me because I was sure that one day my ignorance would be uncovered and there would be nothing that made me special, or worth caring for.

I found the senior part of Durlston Court harder to deal with than the lower school. Durlston had only recently started to admit female students, and although Jane had lots of friends who moved up from the lower school, I was the only girl in the whole of my year group.

The boys' boisterousness made me more timid than ever. I had no idea what to say to any of them and they sensed my weakness and fear and teased me relentlessly. It didn't help that I was praised endlessly for my academic ability, and invariably received the class prize each term, a beautifully bound book.

One day, I was told that I would be going to the cinema to watch Star Wars with a group of older boys and the Headmaster, Mr Onslow. It was supposed to be a special treat, but I was terrified at the prospect. He made sure I sat next to him, so the boys didn't pick on me for once, but I still couldn't relax or concentrate on the film, just sat in my seat hoping it would be over as quickly as possible. I was embarrassed, sensing that Mr Onslow knew about my distraction and was puzzled by it, and by me.

Mr Ransome was my English teacher, and I worshipped the ground he walked on. He protected me, boxing the ears of one boy he spotted pushing me over. He encouraged me to read, letting me help him unpack boxes of books that were delivered to the library. He made me laugh, horsing around in the classroom. He used to come into our lessons smoking a cigarette, then he'd throw the butt out of the window. A few minutes later, he'd glance out, pretend to see the cigarette ends for the first time, and demand to know which of the boys had been smoking. This performance cracked me up every time.

One day he brought in his daughter, a tiny toddler whom he stood on his desk for us to admire. I was surprised by how jealous I felt. I think it was the first time that I really felt the injustice of my existence. Why should this child have the best man in the world to look after her, when I only had my old, angry father? I knew, of course, that I could do nothing about any of it, except endure it.

Being a child was no fun, in my experience. To the outside world, it might have looked like the Gillett children led a privileged existence, attending private schools, living in a mansion in the countryside. But my nerves and awkwardness, caused or exacerbated by the unpredictable and volatile atmosphere at home, made my life a misery.

At least at school I could keep my mind occupied by studying. When I was immersed in learning I could forget about the worrisome situation at Harrow Lodge. At Durlston Court my hard work was recognised. I was told that I had a particular ability for Latin, and was moved up to join the boys in the year group ahead of me. These boys were even worse than the ones in my usual class. They hated me, thought I was stuck-up and that I was going to show them up. They needn't have worried because I really understood very little Latin. I could only think that my teachers must have mistaken my silence in the lessons for understanding, and I was sure that my ignorance would be unmasked at any moment. I kept my head above water, but only by concentrating very hard in class.

Durlston Court had a small chapel, and a full-time vicar in residence. He was a friendly man, very hospitable, and kept a soda stream machine in the little wooden hut by the chapel where he spent the time between lessons and services. For this reason, he had lots of visitors. I didn't need the inducement. I was already a devout child. At Harrow Lodge I had a children's Bible, which I'd read many times when I ran out of other books, and I knew all the stories by heart.

I loved handsome, bearded Jesus. I loved the stability, the reassurance, of faith. I liked singing and praying in chapel. My dearest wish was to become a vicar myself, although that was an avenue that was not available to females, for reasons I did not understand but fully accepted.

The main difficulty I had at school was my inability to communicate. I had no voice. Or rather, I had a perfectly good voice but found it impossible to speak. This reached ridiculous lengths one evening, when something had happened at home and I couldn't be collected on time. I was told I had to stay and eat dinner with the boarders, which struck terror into my heart. I was shown to a table, where I sat in silence not knowing what to say to any of the boys around me. I was ravenous and there were grapes on my side plate, but we had been told not to eat until the masters arrived. Butterflies fought with hunger in the pit of my stomach.

The boy next to me was eyeing the grapes on my plate. 'Hey, do you want your grapes?' he asked. Of course I want them, idiot, I replied silently. But he kept on, 'Do you want them? Do you want them?'

I hated speaking aloud. I always thought I was going to say the wrong thing. I stayed quiet but he kept repeating the same question. 'No,' I said eventually, realising I had made a mistake as soon as the word came out of my mouth. What I meant was, 'No, you can't have them.' But what he heard was, 'No, I don't want them,' and before I could force any more words out of my stupid mouth, he scooped the prized fruit from my dish, and added it to the pile on his own plate. I watched helplessly, resigning myself to my fate as usual.

At that moment Andrew Ransome arrived to preside over our table. He intoned grace in his lovely drawl, 'For what we are about to receive, may the Lord make us truly grateful.' I loved his voice. Every word he said made life seem easier, made my worries seem irrelevant.

Now that the master had arrived, we could eat. But before anyone could start, Mr Ransome glanced around the table and took in the fact that something was wrong. 'Louise has no grapes,' he said. 'Don't you like grapes, Louise?'

'I do,' I said truthfully. I didn't explain what had happened. It would have taken too many words and I could only speak in monosyllables at the best of times.

'Louise has no grapes,' the teacher repeated. 'Each of you must give her some grapes from your plates.'

Every boy around the table stared at me with disbelief and hatred. Reluctantly, each of them took a few grapes from their plate and passed them down the table. Mr Ransome was satisfied that justice had been done, and our dinner began at last.

I was mortified. I was so embarrassed that I wanted to disappear into the ground and never return. I don't know how I managed to eat my food without choking on it, but somehow I survived that meal.

I was at Durlston Court for five, long years, before I made a friend, a new girl, Lorna, who singled me out for company because I was the only other female in the year group. Lorna was blonde, bubbly and an instant hit with the boys. They badgered her to play kiss chase, but she said that she would only play if I was allowed to join in.

I would rather not have been invited. Pretending to run away from boys who never chased me, so that they could get on with the real business of chasing Lorna, was my least favourite activity in the world. The charade went on for weeks because I never found the words to object. It was excruciating.

One terrible day it all came to a head. I had got to school and realised that I had forgotten to put any knickers on. I was completely bare under my skirt. I confided my very serious problem to my friend Lorna, who promised faithfully, crossing her heart and hoping to die, that she wouldn't tell a soul.

At playtime, it seemed that I was surrounded by every single boy at the school, all demanding to know whether it was true that I was wearing no knickers. I was confounded, until I saw Lorna standing at the edge of the circle, smiling sweetly.

71

Thank goodness, I'd had a brainwave. During morning lessons I'd remembered my navy-blue gym pants, and had put them on before playtime. I didn't say a word to the howling group of boys, just carefully lifted a corner of my skirt and showed them the edge of my pants. They all wandered off, disappointed at the lack of drama. And I never spoke a word to Lorna again.

I was good at sports, probably because I was permanently on edge, alert. I was in the school hockey and netball teams. To be honest, it would have been difficult not to be selected, since there were so few girls at Durlston. I was also a strong swimmer. One day, I was walking alone past the big, outside pool when a boy loomed up and threatened to throw me into it. I wasn't scared at all and, although I didn't say anything, I looked him straight in the eyes. If he threw me into the water, I knew he'd be in a lot more trouble than I would be. He thought better of it, and wandered off confused, looking for someone else to bully.

One day I met a new teacher in the hallway outside my classroom. He seemed to know me already, because he called me by my name when he stopped to greet me. He was slim and well-dressed in an old-fashioned but stylish suit and introduced himself as Mr Shelley. He also introduced me to his wife, Mary, who was beautiful. She had long, dark hair and wore an ankle-length dress.

Mr Ransome then turned up and I told him I had met the new English teacher. 'What new teacher?' he asked. I told him about Mr Shelley and his wife, who was going to teach French but he looked mystified. 'Where did you see this man, Louise?'

72

'They both came down the stairs, over there.' I started to point down the corridor, but stopped in embarrassment when I realised there were no stairs in that direction. Mr Ransome looked at me strangely. He clearly didn't believe that I had seen anyone, and now I wasn't sure of it either. I never saw Mr Shelley or his wife Mary again.

I felt so apart, so alien at school. My shyness and silence marked me out as different and I always felt plain and ugly. When I look at photos of the Durslton Court hockey or netball teams now I see an ordinary little girl, short-haired like most other girls in the 'seventies, pretty enough for a nine-year-old. But that wasn't how I felt at all. I hated being at school and all I wanted was to be left alone, to read books. A different life existed in books, a happy life. I could relax between the pages of a book. I could forget myself.

My time at Durlston ended suddenly. Jane and I were both surprised when our father unexpectedly announced that we would be leaving to join our elder sisters at their boarding school. Ian Onslow, the Headteacher, was not pleased. He begged my father to let me stay at Durlston. 'If you leave Louise here, she will have passed all her O levels by the time she's thirteen,' he said. My father wasn't interested. His word was law, which in this instance meant that, as he decreed, I was heading to Roedean School for Young Ladies.

12
Roedean School for Young Ladies

Roedean turned out to be not only my new home, but my redemption. I was sent there in October 1978 when I was nearly ten years old, at the start of the Michaelmas Term, which I had previously known as Christmas Term. I thrilled to the new language. I was hyped up with excitement from all the Enid Blyton stories of boarding school I had read, about life at Malory Towers and St Clare's.

I had reservations, of course. I was not altogether pleased to leave my home and I knew I would miss my little dog Buster, my mother, and Harrow Lodge itself. But I did enjoy the preparations. I was especially happy about the trip with my mother and sister to Harrods in London, where exorbitant amounts of money were spent on my new school uniform, navy pinafore dresses and blue striped shirts, PE kit, gym kit… I particularly loved my trunk, a large, navy blue affair with gold studs, into which all my new belongings were fitted.

We lived in ostensible luxury at Harrow Lodge, but I had never been over-burdened with personal possessions. I was sent to boarding school with what I needed and no more, but to me these were riches. I was particularly taken with my new jeans, which fitted perfectly because they had never belonged to anyone before me. The jeans were for Saturdays, when we would be allowed to wear them with our school uniform tops for morning lessons.

I took one dress for Sundays, when we were allowed to wear our own clothes. As it turned out, I only ever owned this one dress in all the time I spent at Roedean, but nobody ever commented on the fact, or indeed appeared to notice. The dress was made of soft, brown cotton with a light floral design and long sleeves, and I adored it.

I arrived at Roedean with high hopes, and for once I was not disappointed. From my first day there, I fitted in to my new school effortlessly. I was at the top of my class academically, but this was a privilege that I had already learned to take for granted at Durlston Court, and it didn't matter much to me.

What I found much more exciting, and infinitely stranger, was that I suddenly had more friends than I could find time for. My company was highly sought after for games of jacks, handstand competitions and all sorts of other entertainment that we devised for ourselves in our free time. I excelled at all of it.

It felt as though I had entered a parallel world, a dream-state. I was the captain of the sports teams, the person who chose the other members, instead of the person smarting with humiliation at the back of the crowd, knowing she would be the last to be selected.

I was the instigator of midnight feasts, the organiser of strange events like days when we all wore our hair in two bunches, or plaited it overnight so that we came down to breakfast looking like frizz balls. Suddenly I was the most popular girl in school, and I didn't have a clue why.

At first I thought it must be a trick or an illusion, but I soon learned to relax and revel in the attention. For the first time I could remember, I was truly happy.

13
Prize-giving

The contrast between my life at home and my life at
school was mind-boggling. At Roedean, I was treated as
an individual, respected, appreciated and rewarded for
hard work. Any punishments were rational and
reasonable, not that I ever incurred much in the way of
punishment since I was by nature an obedient child. As
my change of circumstances seeped into my
consciousness, I felt an overwhelming sense of relief
about being away from home. I looked forward to letters
from my mother, but experienced a twinge of
conscience when they arrived and I realised that in fact I
was perfectly happy without her.

One day I, and the other new girls, spent an
afternoon in the changing room, writing in felt-tip pen
on our new canvas book satchels. I copied the others,
used my best handwriting to inscribe 'I love Mummy
and Daddy' and 'Home for Ever'. I laboured over the
deceitful artwork. I, who was so scrupulous with the
truth. I looked up to see the Junior House headmistress,
Miss 'Bobby' Robinson, watching me as I wrote. I
sensed that she was somehow aware of my duplicity,
although I knew she could not possibly be.

I embellished my hymn book in the same
manner, decorating it with a paper cover patterned with
hearts and flowers, writing more declarations along the
lines of 'Home is Great', then sealing it all in with strips
of Sellotape, immortalising my lies. The other girls did
exactly the same.

There was a strict routine to life at Roedean. We got up
at 7am and studied from 9am until 5.45pm, with breaks

for lunch and play. Bedtime was at 7pm, but as we progressed to the next year group, we were entitled to an additional 15 minutes before bed. At the age of 12, I was still going to bed at 7.30 every evening.

Alongside the usual lessons, and PE, we were taught to knit and crotchet and play draughts, chess, bridge and so on. The pursuits of young ladies, probably unchanged since the founding days of the school. As a concession to modern times, we were allowed to watch television on a Thursday evening, but only two programmes: Blue Peter and Top of the Pops. The latter was closely monitored and the television promptly switched off if anything came on that was deemed unsuitable viewing for young ladies. Bobby Robinson had an inbuilt, finely tuned unsuitability monitor. Pan's People were turned off immediately. Bucks Fizz survived, by the skin of their teeth.

We had speech training classes too. I was interested to find out what these lessons were about, because we'd had nothing like them at Durlston Court. They turned out to be something and nothing. The lessons were taken in our large common room, where we clustered on the floor, near the piano. The teacher was young and pretty, and the lessons were pleasant enough, but took no particular form. Mostly she just spoke to us or played tunes that she liked, some of them slightly odd choices for young ladies.

We obediently sat still, as we had been taught, but personally I was confused as I listened yet another time to the lyrics of one of her favourites: 'Suicide is painless/It brings on many changes/And I can take or leave it as I please/And you can do the same thing if you please'. Was our teacher depressed, I wondered? Or was she trying to tell us something? Whatever it was all about, I was sure Bobby Robinson would not approve.

Living conditions were basic. My dormitory consisted of rows of cubicles, separated by partition walls that stopped short of the ceiling, like the ones in public lavatories. There were no doors, only curtains that you could pull closed at night, like those around the beds in hospital wards. There was only room in each cubicle for one small child, a bed, a chest of drawers and a tiny built-in wardrobe.

I didn't mind. I was fast learning that happiness was not connected to the ownership of things, or the possession of money. Indeed, I thought perhaps the reverse applied. My father was certainly a living example of how money did not maketh the man.

We had very little freedom. We lived by the clock and the book, with regimented lesson times and countless school rules. We were allowed to bathe and wash our hair only on certain days and at pre-arranged times. There were regular fire-drills, and if these happened to occur at bath time or when we were fast asleep, we were expected to go straight down to the playground to be counted, although this meant we had to standing outside shaking with cold, in our night clothes or wrapped in towels. We accepted this, of course, and waited patiently in line until the building was checked and the fire officer in charge declared it safe for us to return to the building.

I didn't resent any of it. Rather, I thrived on the structure and organisation. It could not have been more different from my unpredictable existence at home. I even learned to play the piano. I had no real ear for music but learned how to read it by rote, and found that by dint of regular practice I could satisfactorily reproduce the scales and pieces of music and pass the exams.

I didn't excel at these exams and never gained more than a 'merit' because I lacked the confidence or ability to sing out loud, which was a necessary part of the tests. However, I still did well enough to win the school prize for the most 'commendations', which amounted to house points, for both music and academic work, nearly every week.

The prizes were small pictures in frames, awarded by the Head of the whole school, John Hunt, at a ceremony each Saturday, which the winner kept for one week until the next prize-giving. I was given these pictures so often that I practically assumed ownership of them. And the peculiar thing about this was that the other girls not only did not mind, they respected me for it. It was hard to believe, at times, that my status among my peers had changed so much, and so suddenly.

My time at Roedean was a true golden era. At last, I was living the life of a child, carefree and unburdened. I loved every moment of it. At the end of my first year, my parents received a letter from the teaching staff, advising that I should be moved to the academic year above. This was vetoed on the grounds that it would have been awkward for Jane to have a younger sister in the same class. I was glad. I had no desire to stretch my academic capabilities. I remembered the humiliation of the Latin lessons at Durlston Court when I'd been moved up to the older boys' class. I was happy with my friendship group at Roedean. I did not want to upset the balance in any way.

14
Judaism

I rarely saw Jane at school, except for the occasions
when our mother drove to Brighton to take us both out
for the day. These 'exeats', as they were called,
happened three or four Saturdays each term. Mum took
us to the Old Ship Hotel in town for drinks, or to wander
around the shops in the old Lanes. When the film
'Grease' came out, she took us to see it at the cinema on
several exeats in a row. It seems strange to remember
how smokers sat on the left-hand side of the cinema.
This, of course, was where Jane and I sat with our
mother, transfixed on the scenes before us.

Occasionally our father came on the exeat visits,
and when this happened Mum brought Stephen too, and
we spent all our time in the Old Ship Hotel. We ate large
meals in a private dining room while my father
reminisced about his school days at Brighton College,
when his own father had taken him to the Old Ship on
exeat days.

I worried about my mother's journey from
Harrow Lodge to Brighton. It was a family joke, or at
least my father found it funny, that over the years mum
had written off several expensive Jaguars and Rolls-
Royces on these journeys. In one accident my sister
Mandy, who was in the front passenger seat, had her
front teeth knocked out and was taken to Harley Street
for pioneering surgery to re-root them. The possibility of
my mother hurting herself on the drive to visit us at
school began to haunt me.

Around this time, my mother decided to convert to
Judaism. I was surprised by this, since neither she nor

my father had ever seemed interested in religion, but she persevered with the long and complicated process of conversion, learning the rudiments of the Hebrew language and the rules and history of the Jewish religion.

Eventually, Mum convinced a board of Rabbis that her new beliefs were genuinely held and she was officially accepted as a Jew. She also converted each of her children. I was given a Jewish name, Yisraelia, and a certificate to declare my new religious affiliation.

I was puzzled but compliant, accepting the decision because it seemed so important to our mother. As time went on, I became proud to be Jewish, and devoured everything I could find in print about the history of the Jews. I read countless books about the Holocaust and quickly developed a sense of responsibility to the members of my new tribe, who had suffered so greatly in the past.

Being officially Jewish meant that we no longer ate bacon, and on Yom Kippur we fasted at school, or attempted to. Nobody seemed to notice or care, since Roedean was multi-cultural. Jane and I still attended chapel but were not expected to take communion.

When we were at home, we attended the Reform synagogue in Bournemouth on Saturdays. On Sunday mornings, Jane, Stephen and I also went to Sunday School there, which consisted of the Rabbi and some of his assistants teaching us Hebrew. I enjoyed learning a new alphabet, the new sounds and shapes of the letters. The words were read differently, from left to right, and I felt I was learning a sort of code, that I had gained access to privileged information.

At the end of my first summer term at Roedean, we went

on a family holiday to Israel. There were seven of us: our parents, Mandy and Belita, who were sixteen and seventeen, and we three younger children. My father was officially embracing his Jewish roots.

We stayed at the Sheraton in Tel Aviv, where we spent a lot of time by the hotel swimming pool. Mandy and Belita competed with my Mum to get the darkest tan, by means of liberal applications of Bergasol oil. Mars Bars cost three pounds each, which we three youngsters found an endlessly amusing, although in theory we grasped the concept that three Israeli pounds equated to one of ours.

Jane, Stephen and I shared a large room and were mostly left to our own devices. We made liberal use of room service, which we regarded as a brilliant innovation. My father was, for once, in a good mood. He announced one day that a miracle had occurred, that he had felt his back pain completely disappear when he was standing at the Wailing Wall. I thought there were better candidates than my dad who could benefit from a medical miracle but still, I hoped for all our sakes that it was true, because life was so much better for everyone when he was happy.

15
Halcyon Days

I believed that these halcyon school days would last forever. As time passed, I relaxed into a sense of wellbeing. I kept up an impeccable academic record, improved my sporting and swimming skills, and enjoyed the social life at Roedean.

The young ladies of Junior House were carefully guarded. We were only occasionally allowed to leave the school, when we were taken out by the teaching staff for short walks, either to the nearby village of Rottingdean or to the beach. Roedean was situated on the cliff top above Brighton Marina. A private tunnel ran from the school grounds down to a secluded part of the beach, which meant that on our visits there we encountered few people from the town.

On one of our walks, we almost fell over a man who was laying naked on a thin towel which he had spread across the stony beach. We all stood around goggling and giggling until Miss Coulter, our deputy headmistress, caught on to the cause of our amusement and bustled over, bristling with indignation.

'Kindly cover yourself up, young man,' she demanded, although he looked a long way from young to us. 'There are young ladies in the vicinity.'

What Miss Coulter didn't know was that the area had recently been declared a naturist zone and the offending gentleman was simply exercising his democratic rights. Grumbling about this, he obliged her by covering his private parts with a newspaper until we had all passed by, by which time we had already seen it all anyway.

It was on one of our trips to the beach that my

83

best friend Nicky and I decided to capture some crabs and take them back to the school to keep as pets. We stored them in soap dishes on the windowsills of our cubicles and promptly forgot about them. A few days later, we found the dishes empty in our rooms – Matron didn't say a word, so we assumed that the creatures had somehow managed to dislodge the lids and escape. We never saw our pet crabs again. Perhaps they or their descendants are still scuttling about somewhere in that august educational establishment on the Brighton cliff top.

As replacements, Nicky and I decided to keep pet woodlice, this time in our geometry cases, which we lined with moist tissue to keep the creatures as comfortable as possible. We took our new pets everywhere with us that week, until on Sunday in chapel they escaped. I was caught by Miss Robinson crawling on my hands and knees between the pews.

'What do you think you are doing Louise?' Bobby demanded. She was bemused to hear that the best behaved pupil in her extremely well-managed part of the school was, 'Looking for my pet woodlouse, which has escaped.'

The following morning I was hauled up before the revered Headmaster of Roedean School, Mr John Hunt, whom I had previously only encountered when collecting my regular weekly prizes. I was shaking with fear as I waited outside the office to be admitted to his presence. However, faced with a child who was clearly scared stiff, never mind mad enough to want to keep a pet woodlouse, the venerable headteacher only seemed to be faintly amused.

I was sure I detected a twinkle in his eye as he

enquired, 'Are you aware that you have done something wrong, Louise?'

'Oh yes, sir!' I agreed readily.

'And are you sorry?'

'Oh, I am sir!'

'Well, that's fine then. Off you go!'

Not needing to be told again, I flew from the scene of my disgrace, racing away up the corridor at top speed.

16
An Exhibition

Of course this silly, happy episode of midnight feasts, fun and high larks and justice for all could not last forever. I was nearing the end of my time at Junior House when the denouement came.

It was the second term of my third year at boarding school. I was twelve years old, and now I was not only head of dormitory, keeper of all the school prizes and valued member of all the school sports teams, I was also the head of Austen, my school house. The houses were neatly named after famous women – Jane Austen, Elizabeth Fry, Florence Nightingale and Sarah Siddons. Austen was the 'Red' house. (At Durlston I was also in the 'red' team – I had worn a red tie to denote my membership of St George's house, as opposed to St Andrew's (blue) St David's (yellow) or St Patrick's (green).)

That Easter, when Jane and I went home for the half-term holiday, Harrow Lodge was in upheaval. My father's temper was fouler than usual, and everyone was in a flap. Worst of all, our little Jack Russell terriers, Buster and Scrapper, had vanished. We were told that they had been fighting with Grace and Ghia, the new Alsation guard dogs, and they had been given away. We were assured they had gone to a good home, and now lived in a caravan with their new family. Jane and I never saw our pets again, never had a chance to say goodbye. We were devastated.

More bad news followed. We were told that my father's financial situation was now dire. When we were due to return to school after half-term, he announced that he could no longer afford to pay the fees. Jane and I were to be withdrawn from school as soon as possible.

At Roedean, I was quickly entered for a scholarship test as an internal candidate. However, during the exam my confidence plummeted. I noticed one girl who had come to sit the scholarship from another school, and I compared myself unfavourably with her – how neat and tidy she looked, how articulate she was. How normal and nice both her accompanying parents seemed too – not a cigarette in sight. I felt I had no chance of passing the test – I realised that I didn't belong at Roedean.

I sat a written paper, but then struggled to express myself at all in the oral part of the exam. I was dumbstruck, staring at my questioner as if she could understand what I was thinking, as if she knew how desperately I wanted to stay at this school. I couldn't respond to a single one of her questions. I was taken from the room in the middle of the exam and removed to the school sanatorium, where I was kept quietly for a few hours.

To my astonishment, I was awarded a prize after all. This was not a scholarship, which would have entitled my father to a reduction of school fees, but an exhibition, which meant that I could stay on indefinitely at Roedean without any payment at all. My teachers at the Junior School must have vouched for my ability, despite the fiasco of the oral examination.

But my father announced that it would be unfair to Jane if I was allowed to remain at boarding school and she was not. Her opinion on this was not canvassed. I was not surprised by my Dad's ruling – I had felt for some time that doom was imminent – but I did feel a strong sense of injustice and powerlessness.

We only had a few weeks left at Roedean until the Easter holidays. I didn't see Jane during this time. She was in the Senior part of the school by then so we rarely encountered each other. Jean Summers, our housekeeper, had recently given me an autograph book. The first signature was that of her son, Andy Summers, who was a musician, the guitarist in the rock band The Police. All my friends wrote their farewells in that book, and I determined tearfully that I would keep it close to me forever.

On the Saturday morning that I was due to leave Roedean, an end-of-term prize giving was held. Austen won the most team points and there was a new prize, for the most house points won by an individual. It was a silver cup, and my name was engraved on it. Mr Hunt handed it over to me formally, and then I handed it back to Miss Robinson. I never saw it again.

In the afternoon, my mother arrived to collect me. My possessions were packed in my trunk. I roller skated around the school hall with my friends. I loved that hall, its beautiful wooden balcony at one end and large stage at the other. It was the venue for happy occasions – assemblies and prize-givings. On Saturdays after lunch we were allowed to choose sweets from our tuck boxes, tins that were kept under lock and key in the area behind the stage.

My mother and Bobby Robinson stood watching me roller skate around the school hall. They didn't speak much to each other. And I didn't say much either, as I left the beloved building that had been more of a home to me than the place where my family lived. A formal goodbye to my teachers, a final wave to my friends, and we were in the car and gone.

I was always a quiet child, at least in the company of adults, but from that point I spoke even less. I was overwhelmingly aware of the lack of power I had in my own life. Whatever, I said, decisions would be made for me, and I would be forced to comply. So what was the point of ever sharing my views?

I had found my voice at Roedean, but as my mother drove her elegant, lethal car down the sweeping driveway, away from the place I loved, I left that voice behind, along with a whole host of emotions. I switched a part of myself off so I could bear the life that lay ahead, as Jane and I were driven away from our old school, towards an uncertain future. Goodbye, dear Roedean. Goodbye friendship, fun, safety, security.

17
885 Christchurch Road

Harrow Lodge had been sold, so Jane and I didn't get to say goodbye to our beloved Hampshire home either. Myself, Belita, Mandy, Jane, Stephen, our parents and Grace and Ghia the Alsation dogs, relocated to a maisonette above a small shop in Pokesdown, one of the most run-down areas of Bournemouth.

My father christened the shop 'Victorian Paintings Limited'. I thought the name had a ring to it, although it was a little puzzling because he sold mostly jewellery and some antiques, but never paintings. But I had long since given up expecting anything to make sense.

I was lucky to have spent almost three years at boarding school. It was a time of unmarred happiness. If I'd progressed to the senior school my unusual home background might have marked me as different, but in Junior House we were all friends, and the whole experience had been wonderful.

But the good times had melted away. It was a huge culture shock. There were seven members of our family in the smoky flat above the shop at 885 Christchurch Road, which meant that there was no space for a sitting room, although in any case we were not the sort of family to have gathered in one.

Belita spent her days working alongside my father in the jewellery shop, a miserable occupation for a seventeen-year-old girl. Mandy started her A levels at Brockenhurst college. She was only fifteen when she left Roedean, and she had already passed thirteen O levels.

Stephen had been attending a private day school, Edinburgh House, but he and Jane were both sent to the local comprehensive, Beaufort School. It had a terrible reputation and neither of them flourished there.

I passed the eleven plus exam, and went to the local grammar school, Bournemouth School for Girls. It was the beginning of the summer term, 1982. The girls in my new class already knew each other well and as a new girl I was automatically an outsider. Like my siblings, I missed my old school and my old friends, but none of us had any choice except to get on with things. We never complained to our parents or to anybody else. There would have been no point.

Jean Summers stayed on as our housekeeper at '885', as we referred to our new home. She stayed to care for our mother, really. Mum wasn't physically or mentally capable of dealing with the mountains of washing and the back-breaking duties of cleaning and cooking. Jean, little bird of a woman as she was, did all the hard work, and did it willingly. She was spared from the brunt of Dad's moods, because even he knew that Jean was special. As mother to an international rock star she outclassed us all, and she could have retired in style.

Jane and I shared an attic bedroom above the Pokesdown shop. Mandy had her own room next door. Jane insisted on watching terrifying late-night films on the small black and white TV in our room. The films prevented me sleeping and gave me nightmares when I did drop off. Jane laughed at my fears and teased me mercilessly but when she was in a good mood, she was great company.

We would often look out of our bedroom

window at the 896 Coffee Bar opposite, where long-haired, rough-looking men and youths disappeared down steep stairs to hidden rooms below. We threw small pieces of paper or other rubbish out of our window at them to get their attention, and then hid when they looked to see where it had come from. We envied their freedom and longed to be allowed to look into the 896 Coffee Bar for ourselves, but were too well aware of the reaction we'd receive from our father if we asked.

We seldom saw our elder sisters, or our mother. One evening I had to go downstairs to use the toilet. It was past my bedtime, and Mum was huddled in the kitchen with Mandy and Belita, deep in conversation. She scolded me sternly for using the bathroom so late and told me to go straight back to bed.

I did what I was told, but I still desperately needed a wee. I ventured downstairs again, but this time my mother really shouted at me. She thought I was trying to eavesdrop on her conversation with my sisters. I was taken aback because Mum was so rarely cross.

Without using the bathroom, I hurried back upstairs and told Jane what had happened. I tried to sleep but was desperate for a wee. I tried to ignore the feeling, but it only intensified. I didn't know what to do. My mother had screeched at me twice already, and told me not to dare come down again. I didn't dare. On the other hand, I had to wee. Minutes ticked by. My bladder was agony. I appealed to Jane, and she came up with an immediate solution. 'Wee in your bed,' she said. 'That'll show her.'

The idea horrified me. I was twelve years old, and had never wet the bed in my life, or at least not as far as I could remember. But I was petrified of what my mother might do or say if I went down to use the toilet again.

Eventually I had no option. I wet my bed because I could hold myself in no longer, and then cried with misery and shame. Jane went downstairs gleefully to tell our mother, who came up to change the bed. It was sodden, and of course Mum was furiously angry.

18

99 Red Balloons

Mandy was out a lot at college but when she was at home, she talked to me about what was happening in her life, and occasionally lent me books to read. I felt sorry for her. Most of my dad's bad temper seemed to be taken out on her, and he was frequently in her room shouting and swearing about some imaginary offence. Jane and I often huddled together, anxiously listening to the sound of his footsteps as he stomped up the stairs to yell at our beloved big sister, and then stomped away again, leaving the faint sounds of her sobs behind.

This culminated in a particularly awful episode when Dad ordered Mandy to leave home. She went to stay with Jean and her family and never came back, moving on from Jean's house to share with some friends from college. Nonetheless, she gained good grades in her A levels, and because she was still only seventeen, officially too young to start university, she decided to travel for a year, having been awarded a place to study law at the London School of Economics on her return.

Before she left the country, Mandy took Jane, Stephen and I to the park, and photographed us on the swings and slides. I suppose she was storing up memories. In those pictures I looked young, thin, worried. Caught in action on my way down the slide, my expression was serious. I never smiled in those days.

Mandy stopped by the shop at 885 on her way to the airport, to say goodbye before she left. The taxi driver revved his engine loudly, but he needn't have been concerned. She got short shrift. Another father might have been sad to see his daughter go abroad alone, but ours refused even to say goodbye. Instead, he stood on the pavement outside his shop and shouted obscenities at his seventeen-year-old daughter in the street, continuing to yell them after her departing taxi.

I understood exactly why Mandy left home, and I would have done the same if I was old enough. Like our older brothers and sisters, who gradually severed contact with what was left of our family as my father's behaviour became more outrageous, she was better off away from the mess that passed as the Gillett family life.

Jane and I still shared a room. We didn't want to encroach on the space Mandy had left, and perhaps we also sensed that there was safety in numbers. We used our room as a refuge and spent a lot of time on the stairs, alert to the sounds below before we judged whether it was safe to venture down. Was our father home, or was he out?

We listened to the radio on the steep attic stairs because it was the only place where we could get a good enough reception. This was our teenage soundtrack: ranting and bellowing from below, the strains of 99 Red Balloons sickly sweet in the air nearby. Nobody in our family had much money, time or energy for pop music though, or any other hobbies. All our resources and attention went towards our survival.

19
Bournemouth School for Girls

Emotionally, I plummeted a long way in a short time. The decline in my quality of life corresponded with a deterioration in my outlook and attitude. Theoretically, I knew I was lucky to have a place at the grammar school. Jane and Stephen were badly bullied at Beaufort School, whereas my peers at Bournemouth School for Girls were mostly friendly, polite and hard-working.

However, they were also mostly happy, which meant that I had nothing in common with them. I quickly became disillusioned with the school, too. The academic standard was much lower than I was used to, and the authorities refused to put me in the year above my age group, even though my October birthday meant I was already one of the oldest in the school year and even though I had been in the class above my age since I was five.

I could do the work with my eyes shut. We were learning beginner's Latin and French, for example, and I had already been studying both subjects for eight years. I persuaded my mother to object to the school about the standard of work, and she was assured that if I did well in my end of year exams I would be moved up. I duly got A* for every subject, but was then told that it would be impossible to move me.

I was bored and resentful. I was also unhappy and had no friends. I couldn't find anyone who was like me, or who I was prepared to like.

Until I met Debbie. Debbie was a scoundrel, but she was great fun. Her way of opening the conversation was to ask what bands I liked, which had me stumped and panicking. Jane and I were given record players when we were young, but we never had pocket money to buy records, so we didn't get the chance to develop our musical tastes. In fact, the only records I ever owned were 'Puff the Magic Dragon', Rod Stewart's 'Sailing' and 'Underwater', an album by the Boomtown Rats, from which I memorised every depressing word.

However, I knew enough about the way things worked to recognise that Debbie's question about pop music was a test to see how cool I was, and I knew too that I was going to fail. We were walking around the back of the main school building as we talked. It was a warm spring morning, and I saw other girls sitting in small groups round the nooks and crannies of the building, chatting. My blood ran cold. For once I had company that I was enjoying, and I knew that I was about to lose my grip on it.

I tried to dredge the name of some acceptable group from my memory. The Beatles, whose music I loved to play on my recorder at Roedean? No, they wouldn't do. Not trendy enough. At last I remembered my trump card, and played it. My favourite band was The Police, of course, and I knew the members personally (that was an exaggeration, but I had seen Andy once when I visited Jean's house, and I would have met Sting and Stewart too, if only they had been there.)

Debbie was impressed. I had earned myself a friend. I could relax a little.

20
Smoking

I wrote, intermittently, to my old friends from boarding school. I crafted these letters oddly, or so it seems to me now. I told them all about my new friend Debbie, how I smoked and had boyfriends. I mentioned my earrings. I had three piercings on one side, two on the other. I threw in the fact that I now had 'bra length' hair. I suppose I wanted to sound interesting and happy and was desperate for them not to read between the lines, to realise how lonely and miserable I truly was.

Nobody ever wrote back. Possibly, my letters were never passed on to the young ladies of Roedean by the wise and capable teachers who used to censor our Sunday letters home.

I buried my unhappiness as deeply as I was able. I didn't know how to talk about it, or who I could talk to. My parents were distracted from the effort of getting through their days. Things might not have looked bad from outside the family. My parents never went short of cigarettes and Jean still looked after us. We were warm, fed and always had a roof over our heads.

But my father's forays to the casinos were becoming desperate. It was clear that the money situation was deteriorating fast. My marks at school fell steadily, as I became increasingly disillusioned from having to repeat work I had already done. My academic ability was the one thing I had prided myself on, but I was bored now and refused to make any effort. I was permanently sullen, ignoring any effort by my teachers to draw me out of my shell, and they soon started to ignore me in return.

My friend Debbie was not interested in

schoolwork either. My results remained average or just above and the teachers didn't notice or care that I no longer excelled at my studies, but Debbie's lack of motivation drew more negative attention because it resulted in poor marks, although she didn't seem to mind.

The only subject I bothered to try a little in was English, because it was still my favourite. I was disappointed that we weren't expected to write stories or do any other creative work, but I still made some effort with the essays and comprehensions.

Writing stories and poems was not part of the curriculum, but Debbie and I did it in our own time, blagging blank exercise books from the teachers by pretending that we had filled our subject ones, filling the pages with our schoolgirlish fantasies.

My plots were borrowed directly from the TV show The Professionals because I had a crush on Martin Shaw. Debbie's stories had similar second-hand origins, some of which I was slow to recognise. I was thoroughly impressed by a tale she wrote called 'An American Werewolf in London'. The penny only dropped many years later when I chanced across a film of the same name as Debbie's story, which happened to share exactly the same subject matter.

I read whatever I could find, borrowing books from the school library. It was not a bad library, and I found some classics I hadn't previously encountered and some more modern novels. Once I found an author I liked, I would work my way through all their titles that were stocked by the library.

I would happily have spent every lunch hour and break time in the school library, but this was against the rules. We had to play outside, even when it was raining or freezing cold. I often tried to hide in the library by burying my head in the pages of a book, hoping I would be mistaken for a studious sixth former, but the dinner ladies soon got to know me, and it was never long before I was caught and hustled outside.

I didn't really like socialising with the other girls. I never felt completely comfortable. But when I was forced outside I would find Debbie somewhere in the playground, usually near the bike sheds with the other school rebels and outcasts. She remained my only close friend. Debbie was as plump as I was skinny, as merry as I was miserable. Her skin was as smooth and peach-like as mine was scarred and pitted with acne.

I started smoking, encouraged by my sister Jane, who had recently taken up the habit. Jane realised that if I smoked too then we would share the punishment if we got caught. She threatened to hit me unless I smoked one of her cigarettes, I took the easy option and lit up, and before long I was a nicotine addict.

Although Jane forced me to smoke my first cigarette, I continued to smoke willingly. They tasted awful at first, but I persevered until I acquired a liking for them. Debbie smoked too, and I found it to be a useful social device. It also gave me something to do in my school lunchtimes when I wasn't allowed to read. Cigarettes were a small rebellion, a tiny signal of the turmoil I felt inside. My self-esteem was, by then, non-existent.

Smoking meant I was part of a social group at school, but I felt awkward with the other miscreants, who were mostly older than me and Debbie. One of these older girls took to bullying me, which I found upsetting. I knew I could escape by going somewhere else at lunchtimes, but I didn't know where to go. I considered taking a book to read outside, but there was nowhere to sit down and anyway it was often too wet and cold. Also, I didn't want to be recognised by others as a loner, even if I knew I was one.

The nicotine exerted a strong pull too, although I felt embarrassed to be spending my time in such a stupid way. Our group were often caught smoking and punished for it. The punishment wasn't terrible, only boring. We would have to spend all our break and lunch times for a week inside the school under supervision, untying the knots in the strings that were used to secure exam papers together. At least we were warm and dry.

As time passed, I became addicted to cigarettes. Nicotine held me in thrall. In some ways I didn't completely enjoy the habit. I found the smell noxious and knew that smoking was not good for my health. At home, Mum had two magazines each week and they contained a lot of useful information on living well, particularly about healthy eating. Mum also read The Sun newspaper daily, but this contained no useful information at all. I still read it because I always read anything and everything that I could find.

It wasn't easy to find the money for cigarettes, but Debbie and I worked it out between us. She had a bus pass, but I didn't qualify for one so my mum gave me my bus fare daily. We figured out that if Debbie boarded the bus and then threw her pass out of the window to me, I could use it to get on free. We carried out this ruse with success for a while, although there would be a panic if an inspector boarded. When this happened, I would claim to have lost my ticket or eaten it. As evidence, I would produce from my mouth the soggy remains of some other bus ticket I had found discarded on the floor. Fortunately, our bus did not get inspected often.

The money I saved from bus fares was used to buy cigarettes, which at that time cost about 50p for a packet of ten. Nicotine cravings dealt with.

Eventually, the bus driver (it was always the same driver on our school bus) cottoned on to our ruse and refused to let me board unless I paid. We needed an alternative plan, and we formed one quickly. Debbie's mother made her a packed lunch each day but I had a dinner ticket, a lunch voucher given to pupils from the poorest families. We decided I should sell my ticket to somebody in the lunch queue. It was worth about 70p. Debbie would then share her packed lunch with me, and we'd have funds for our fags later.

I hated selling my dinner ticket. I was always hungry and would have loved a hot meal at lunchtime. Also, I found the process degrading. The other girls had no idea why I would want to skip lunch and most of them wouldn't agree to exchange my dinner ticket for cash. One girl regularly agreed. Diane was as well-brought up as the others, but she was kinder and less judgemental. I am still grateful to her to allowing me to feel human, for not turning down my request with an air of superiority like the others.

The gulf between me and the other girls at the grammar school felt huge. I could have been spotted a mile off, in their groomed and coiffured midst. My school uniform was covered with dog hairs and I stank of cigarettes. I felt like an alien. I was so jealous of the other girls, especially the ones who wore tights or beautiful, clean, long, black socks that pulled up over their knees, so no bare skin showed beneath their regulation pinafores. I owned two pairs of socks, which lasted me through the whole four and a half years at that school. Neither of them was black, and no matter how hard I tried I could never pull them up over my knees.

Perhaps the worst problem was that I was handicapped by an inability to see clearly, both literally and metaphorically. I had struggled with my eyesight for years, but at Roedean I sat at the front of the class because that was where I liked to be, and so I could see the blackboard easily. At Bournemouth School for Girls, I skulked at the back of the room and had to pull the edges of my eyes slantwise with my fingers to see the writing on the board. But I didn't know what good or bad eyesight was, and it didn't occur to me that this was an issue.

However, before long one of the teachers at Bournemouth School for Girls noticed me pulling at my eyelids and squinting, and realised I was as blind as a bat. My mother took me to the optician in Boscombe, where I was issued with a pair of National Health prescription glasses. It was a revelation to be able to see clearly, but I decided the glasses made me look ugly and refused ever to wear them, putting me back at square one. Life was a blur, in so many ways.

21
Child Labour

My horizons were limited. School stood for boredom, but at least I had Debbie to keep me company. Home should be a refuge, but for me it was probably the worst aspect of my life. We children had no command whatsoever over our destinies, and the adults who were supposedly in charge of us were careering out of control.

In the cramped flat above Victorian Paintings Ltd, my father was getting even more restless and grouchy. He spent large tracts of time in the Bournemouth casinos, and any profit the shop made was squandered at the gaming tables there. Dad usually played roulette, occasionally blackjack. The more social card games like poker were anathema to him.

He was a loner, both at work and at leisure. Not that my father considered his casino outings to be a leisure activity. He took his gambling seriously, devising what he called 'systems' to increase the odds of winning. He never realised that gambling was a mug's game.

This perplexed me because of the total lack of logic. My father was once on the other side of the table when he owned his own gambling businesses, so he was well aware that the house always wins. How, then, could he ignore this fact on a daily basis?

He won occasionally but lost far more often, and the losses reflected badly on his mood. Dad had business contacts from the days when he was wealthy, and he could usually find someone from whom he could borrow money for the essentials like food, heating, bills. And, of course, the ubiquitous cigarettes. But we children had few clothes, no pocket money and little hope for our futures. And the poorer the family became, the more unpredictable my father's corresponding moods. His outbursts were increasingly unpleasant. He swore and ranted at all his children for no reason, accusing us of all sorts of impossible offences.

He also used us as unpaid labour. The school holidays were taken up with tedious work, folding sheets of A4 paper and fitting them into envelopes, which we addressed by hand to every household in Bournemouth, working from the phone book.

The missives that we stamped and sent out into the world were Dad's form of advertising, inviting people to come to his shop to sell their unwanted jewellery or antiques. We addressed hundreds, thousands of these mailshots, sitting at tables in the shop for hour after hour working through the phone books. At the end of a full week's work, we were given £25 each (£5 a day) and instructed to take it straight to the Post Office to put into our accounts.

The leaflets resulted in a steady stream of visitors to the shop. Dad bought their goods cheaply, and quickly resold them. But by Monday morning he had invariably squandered the profits, and we would be sent to the Post Office to retrieve our 'wages' and return them to him. We would be 'paid' again on Friday, and again told to put the money straight into our savings accounts, where again it did not stay for longer than the weekend. It was a parody, a comedy of injustice but not surprisingly we didn't see the funny side.

After a while, the stamps stopped and we were instructed to delivered the letters by hand instead. This was an education in itself. I had never seen living accommodation like this before, did not realise how some people had to trek up long corridors in dark, squalid buildings to reach their own front door.

Our father tasked Mum with driving the three of us to a given area each day. She would wait in her car as we ventured out in different directions to post our missives. It was wearisome work. We didn't complain to our mother or discuss it with her. It was just life.

It was becoming clear that our parents could not carry on in this fashion. There was no money to pay the bills. We still had a credit account with the newsagent next door, which kept my parents in cigarettes, but the balance was becoming more and more precarious.

The final straw was when the shop at 885 Christchurch Road was burgled. This happened one evening when my father was closing up. Everybody was out; even Belita, who still lived at home and worked in the shop, was out walking the Alsatians, Grace and Ghia. Normally these animals, guard dogs as well as pets, were walked separately, to maintain security in Belita's absence. This evening she had taken them out together and as soon as she left, two men burst into the shop by the back entrance, brandishing sawn-off shotguns.

My father was in the process of setting the timers on the two large safes in the back room behind the shop. This, in theory at least, was our family lounge room. We never used it because, apart from a television and the safes, it only contained one armchair, a telephone, and the precious collection of every telephone directory in the whole of the United Kingdom, neatly stacked on shelves. These were a work tool since, armed with the addresses of every resident in the country, Dad could send out an awful lot of leaflets.

Behind the lounge was a small utility room, which was Jean Summers' territory. It contained a washing machine, a tumble drier and a lot of Jean Plaidy books, which I felt guilty reading because they had belonged to my Granny and my Mum didn't have many things left to remember her by.

If the robbery had occurred moments later, the thieves would have been thwarted. Once the timers on the safes were set no-one could open them until the morning. The three large men arrived, however, in the nick of time (no pun intended) and quickly rendered Dad helpless, bound and gagged, before making their getaway. They directed a tirade of verbal abuse at my father throughout the proceedings, and when they went they left a trail of faeces behind them, literally smeared all over the shop.

The stock was insured, but the insurance company refused to pay a penny. According to the small print of the policy, my father had failed to take the correct precautions to avoid robbery, because the timers on the safes had not been set. He tried to argue his case with the insurers on the grounds that the robbers must have calculated their crime carefully with the intention of forcing entry during the crucial interval between closing the shop and securing the jewellery. However aggressively Dad harangued the insurers, no payment was forthcoming. The burglary was the bell that tolled for the end of my father's formal attempts at business.

22
RIP, Grace and Ghia

A few weeks later, Belita left home to live with her boyfriend and Jane and I were given her job of walking the dogs each day, on our return from school. Grace and Ghia were still young dogs, around five years old, and very strong. In the previous year they had moved from Harrow Lodge, where they had all the space and freedom they wanted, to the confines of a small shop where they were tethered throughout the day, with only a short walk on a lead to look forward to later. But they were family dogs, and behaved towards us children with impeccable patience and tolerance.

I usually walked Grace, who was slightly smaller than her brother and easier to handle. One day, Jane was busy so I was told to walk Ghia. He was a big, muscular dog, but I was not too worried. I managed to keep him close by pulling firmly on his choke chain as I had been taught.

We'd nearly finished our walk when we passed a small terrier walking along off the lead next to its owner. Ghia suddenly lunged for the other dog and I was unable to hold him back. Through my tears and screams and the shouting of the other dog's owner, I could only sense a blur of snarling and howling. I finally managed to drag the Alsatian away but I was in no doubt about what had happened to the little terrier.

I ran as fast as I could to the house of some neighbours, whose children we knew from school, and begged to be allowed in. I pleaded with them to hide Ghia. I phoned home from there, spurting floods of tears, gasping for breath. I knew it was my fault for not controlling Ghia better. The dog had only been following his instinct, he couldn't help himself. When my mother answered the phone, all I could tell her was that 'Ghia ate a dog'.

The kindly neighbour spoke to my Mum and attempted to calm me down. There was no real chance of hiding Ghia there of course, because everyone in the area knew us, our shop and our dogs. The incident happened in the street practically outside the shop and there were witnesses to tell the distraught owner of the little dead dog exactly who was responsible.

Things happened quickly after that. Within a few days it was clear that Ghia would have to be destroyed and then my father made a terrible announcement. He had decided that Grace would be unhappy without her brother and therefore she should be put down too. Which meant that, although poor Grace was a docile, sweet natured animal who had done no harm, we lost not one family pet but two.

We were all too frightened of my father to challenge him, but we mourned our dogs bitterly. A few months later, Mum had an incredibly brave moment. Dad visited the casino daily, usually as soon as it opened at two o'clock in the afternoon. He often won in these first few hours but could never tear himself away completely. Instead, he brought his winnings home and handed a proportion of the money to my mother, with strict instructions that she should on no account return it to him later in the day.

He then went back to the casino with a smaller sum, to try his luck again. Without fail he would rapidly lose this stake and then come home to rant and rave at my mother until she gave him back the money he had entrusted to her. We all knew she could never stand out against his bullying, but she had to at least try to resist, or pretend to try, or he would blame her when he then lost the whole amount back to the casino.

One afternoon, my father entrusted my mother with £200. Incredibly, she did not keep it safely as he'd admonished, but went out shopping instead. When Dad returned some hours later, penniless, to insist as usual that Mum gave him his money back he found all of us gathered, entranced, around a tiny Alsatian puppy.

This was no ordinary puppy. It was the runt of the litter, which my mother had taken pity on when she was informed by the breeder that it was due to be drowned. The dog was weak and nervous, the biggest coward of an Alsatian that had ever lived. It was frightened of its own shadow, and of every other animal on the planet to boot. We loved it already.

My father exploded with anger. This was the worst kind of disobedience, something he could never have envisaged. My mother had spent his money, the money he needed for ammunition. On an effing dog! The explosion came and every human being in the vicinity quaked and ran for cover. The poor puppy did the same, diving under my parents king-sized bed and refusing to come out.

A few hours later, the house was silent. Jane and I huddled together upstairs, wondering whether my father had killed my mother or the puppy, or perhaps both of them. Eventually a soft knock came at our door and Mum beckoned us downstairs. We all stood in amazement at the threshold to our parents' bedroom, watching our tyrant of a father lying on his huge belly on the floor, half-crawling under the bed, as he attempted by endearments to coax the little dog to come out to him. It was in the same light-hearted spirit that he christened the coward 'Bruiser'.

23
Bruiser

Without Belita to help in the shop, and with no cash flow, my father soon gave up the struggle to keep his shop open. Even without the burglary, we would soon have gone under. Dad's gambling had reached such proportions that the shop could not have sustained his habit for much longer, and the robbery only hastened proceedings. In any case, we were abruptly left penniless and homeless.

Fortunately, my eldest sister Sandra and her husband come to the rescue, buying a three bedroomed property in Wolverton Road in Boscombe, and allowing the family to live there rent free.

Only us three youngest children were now living at home, so by converting the dining room into a downstairs bedroom, which became mine, we each had our own space in the new house. The living room became a lounge-diner. I felt that I had a good deal, room-wise, since I was the furthest away from our parents. The drawback was that my new bedroom had a serving hatch that opened onto the kitchen, meaning that any member of the family who wanted to see or speak to me at any time could open the hatch to do so. I had no privacy whatsoever.

Bruiser, our new dog, moved with us to Wolverton Road. My father developed a game that made the poor thing even more neurotic. He had acquired an old-fashioned hand-held car horn, and when he squeezed the bulb on the end, Bruiser, terrified, would jump up and run from one end of the lounge-dining room to the other, jump onto the sofa, execute a twist and turn, then run back seamlessly to the other end of the room. This afforded my dad no end of amusement and once he started, he carried on with the entertainment for ages. It was one of the few occasions when he ever laughed.

My father always sat in the same old armchair in the corner of the living room, chain smoking. He still drifted off deep in thought and we still had to call him back to reality as the ash hung off the end of his cigarette, waiting to topple. 'Ash! Ash!' we would shout, and he would blearily turn to look at us, then slowly gaze down at his cigarette, the ash falling onto the carpet or his trousers as he moved to look. Some things never changed.

He still wore his Savile Row suits too. I never saw my father dressed in anything other than a three-piece suit, but these were starting to hang off his frame as he became skinnier. He was beginning to cut a pitiful figure, but it was hard to feel sorry for him when we were so scared of him.

The house was filled with cigarette fumes, dog hairs and all the clutter and debris that came with three teenage children and two incapable parents. My mother had never had the knack or the inclination for cleaning, and now that she had no-one to 'do' for her (Jean Summers had finally retired when we moved from the shop), the standard of hygiene in our home was appalling. None of us were particularly bothered. The dirt blended in with the general atmosphere of misery.

I didn't know how my parents managed to make ends meet at all. Neither of them went out to work, so there was no regular income. My father was not cut out for employment and was close to retirement age anyway. He wouldn't tolerate the idea of my mother working either. Why should she, when the casino win that would have us all living in the lap of luxury was around the corner?

In reality, everything was falling apart. When a bill of any kind came through the door, it was a disaster, a state of emergency. The bills would be ignored for as long as possible, but when we were on the verge of having the power cut off, or we needed necessities like school uniforms, or Dad desperately wanted more 'ammunition', he petitioned his old business acquaintances to lend him some cash. He usually succeeded in borrowing the money, on the strength of their sympathy for how far he had fallen.

My mother was a silent presence in the house. She cooked a meal for the family every evening, but most of the time Dad was out at the casino by the time we ate, so she would save his meal for later. She never intervened when he was angry with us.

Jane and I were allowed to attend Pokesdown Youth Club on two evenings each week. One night I came home from the youth club to find that Dad had returned early from the casino. He must have lost heavily, because he was in a foul mood.

My father took exception to my eye shadow. It was green, and I thought it suited me. He obviously didn't, because he started to shout as soon as I walked through the door. 'You look like a fucking prostitute! You look like a fucking witch!' I was thirteen, and scared stiff.

'Get a mirror from your bedroom!' he ordered me. Baffled, I did so. What on earth was coming next, I wondered.

'Now sit there!' he yelled, pointing at the sofa.

'And repeat to yourself, 'I am a witch!''

I sat in the living room while my father glared at me. I watched myself cry into the mirror I was holding, as I chanted obediently, 'I am a witch. I am a witch.' It seemed to go on for ever. Of course, I never believed for a minute that I was a witch, only that he was a nutcase. But that didn't make any difference to the awful reality of my situation.

Another time, he became convinced that Jane and I were lesbians. The 'evidence' was that we often talked to each other, or as he put it, whispered together. It is still painful to remember the desperation, the madness of having to sit quietly and listen to his rantings about lesbian behaviour with my sister. Eventually we were sent to our separate bedrooms and told never to speak to one another again. Stephen took written messages between us for a day or two, as we plotted to tell social services what was happening, and hopefully get ourselves taken into the care of the local authority. We knew two brothers in care, Keith and Sam, and they had a better time of it than we did. They had all the freedom they wanted, and they were given pocket money.

My father soon forgot that Jane and I were not supposed to talk to each other, and things carried on as usual. We would never have called the social services anyway, because we could not have left our mother alone at home with only our father and Stephen for company.

I didn't blame my mum for not trying to stop Dad from behaving like this. I knew as well as she did that her intervention would only have made things worse. She never criticised him when he wasn't there, although she didn't try to explain or defend his behaviour either. She gradually receded into herself, becoming so distant emotionally that she was practically absent.

That Christmas, things hit rock-bottom. Neither my mother nor my father had any friends, and we weren't allowed to have our friends over, so we never had visitors at home. But my father had a few gambling acquaintances, and for some reason one of the men he knew from the local betting shop ended up at our house for Christmas lunch.

Harold was a creep, a sort of yellow decaying Steptoe character. He oozed slime. In fact, if there could be a less attractive man than my father, Harold was that man. However, for some bizarre reason, my mother, sozzled beyond belief (Christmas was the excuse) started flirting with him, in front of my father. The pair of them were drunk and giggling, and then Mum openly began playing footsie with Harold.

He was rapidly ejected from the house by Dad, who then tore a strip off my mother, who was so drunk by then that she paid him no attention at all, although it was dreadful for the rest of us to listen to him berating her.

To top it off, Val Doonican came on the telly. In our house this signalled disaster at the best of times, because he was one of Mum's ex-boyfriends when she was young, back in her nursing days. Whenever Val came on the telly she went all dreamy at the sight of him in his Christmas jumpers, and my Dad seethed with fury.

Val Doonican was bad enough at Christmas when we were well off. He was considerably worse by the time we had sunk to Wolverton Road levels of existence. That Christmas Day was one of those times when I genuinely believed that none of us would survive.

24
Divorce

Luckily, it was only Mum and Dad's marriage that
didn't survive. The end came dramatically one Sunday
morning. I had been staying overnight at my friend
Debbie's house. Mandy, who was living in Israel, had
come back for a visit and had been allowed to stay with
us, so she was in my room. Perhaps it was her presence
that had made my dad so furious. All I knew was that
when I returned from Debbie's in the morning, Mandy
and Jane had barricaded themselves into my bedroom
and were signalling frantically to me through the
window to go away.

My sisters managed to convey that Mum and
Dad had been fighting and that a knife was involved. I
ran for my life and spent the rest of the morning alone
and terrified, imagining a blood bath back at the house.
When Jane caught up with me down at the beach, I was
relieved to find that nobody had been injured after all,
but that Mum was leaving the family home and we
children would be going with her.

It was the beginning of an adventure, albeit a rather
dreary and sordid one. We went to the police station
first, a homeless family with our Alsatian in tow, and
from there we trailed around town with a plethora of
suitcases until we finally found a Bed and Breakfast
establishment that would take us all. Or rather, all of us
except Bruiser, who was banished to kennels to be
further traumatised.

Mandy returned to Israel, and the rest of us spent
a couple of months living in a single room. The first Bed
and Breakfast was grim enough, but then we had to

move to another one that was worse, located next to a sex shop. I can't really remember what we ate or what we all did, stuck together in one room for six weeks. We were certainly not the sort of family to have played board games.

Eventually, my father was evicted from the family home and the rest of us returned there. My mother would not have deliberately made my father homeless, but we had no choice but to return to the Wolverton Road house, because the council would not house us while there was a family home in the picture, and they insisted that my mother instigated legal proceedings to oust my father. He found himself a flat nearby, and a new phase began for our family, one where we children were spared my father's influence all week but had to visit him each Sunday.

These enforced visits were a hideous experience. We went to his flat, Jane, Stephen and I, and sat there in silence while my father ranted about my mother in the craziest and foulest of terms. When he had finished, he would drive us to a local restaurant for lunch, if he happened to have a car at the time. He got through cars rapidly, not because he damaged them but because he sold them if he needed money to gamble.

Dad was on benefits and had no spare money for vehicles. He got the new cars from my older brother, Mike, who brought or sent them to Dad, always complete with a roof rack. Dad insisted on a roof rack because he still occasionally dealt in antiques, pictures and jewellery, or anything he could make a profit from. He was in his mid-sixties by now, but still tireless in his pursuit of money, and would probably be comfortably off if it were not for the demon gambling.

When Dad was between cars, we walked to the restaurant for our Sunday lunch. On one occasion we were passing a petrol station when he suddenly spotted an opportunity. 'Jump into that car!' he shouted, pointing. My brother and sister and I looked back at him blankly. 'That car there!'

The car belonged to a complete stranger. Dad had noticed that the man had failed to lock it when he went to pay for the petrol. 'Get in the fucking car!' he insisted, leading us to it. As the three of us crammed ourselves unwillingly into the back of the car, Dad folded his tall, gangling frame into the front seat.

When the poor man returned to find that an entire family of strangers had established themselves in his vehicle, his face was a picture. He was incredulous. My father, in response, was imperious. 'I am taking my children to lunch,' he declared, 'And we are late. Kindly run us down the road, old chap. What?'

The man was too bewildered to find grounds to object. We travelled to our destination in the free taxi in silence. We children in the back were overcome by embarrassment and horror, but also overtaken by a bizarre urge to laugh at the situation. Thank heavens, my father never repeated that particular trick.

One Sunday as we left his flat, Dad, who did have a car on this occasion, was pontificating on what a great driver he was. He didn't do conversation but he often carried on monologues, and this one was a paean of self-praise, based around the premise that Stirling Moss was a mere amateur in comparison to our father, who had a far superior ability to drive.

We were quiet in the back of the car, resigned to hours of boredom and embarrassment in our father's company before we could escape home. But as he reversed to get out of the parking spot, he hit the car behind. He swore briefly, then continued his discourse about his brilliant driving skills. Then he drove forward again, this time hitting the car in front. With his final manoeuvre, we drove off at last.

Our father had not missed a single beat in his monologue, or adapted its subject matter to take account of current events. He was totally unaware of the stir that he had caused among the three of us, by the sheer irony of the situation. We were all desperate not to catch each other's eyes, in case our giggling became uncontrollable.

The worst aspect of our Sunday visits with my father were the tirades of abuse he directed against our mother. Mum had sent us to see him in good faith, and had no idea of how he behaved, how we had to sit in silence listening to his merciless denouncements of her, agreeing with him when he insisted. He shouted and swore, and all his pronouncements were utterly mad. He was convinced that Mum was, literally, a snake and went to great lengths to convince us of it, citing as evidence the way she moved her arms when she was asleep.

He was truly nutty. I could laugh about his rants later with Jane and Stephen but I found it extremely painful and embarrassing to have to sit and listen to them. I got very upset when I had to see him and begged my mother not to make me go. I could give her no valid reason for not wanting to go, because I couldn't bear to tell her the things he said about her. She continued to force us all to see him every week, and became cross when we tried to wriggle out of it.

Now that she was single, my mum had gone back to work, as a nurse at the local hospital, the Royal Victoria in Boscombe. She was quickly promoted from Staff Nurse to Sister, in charge of the Outpatients Department. I was proud of her. But she found it hard to wake up in the mornings. Every day I made her a cup of tea, brought it to her bedside, tried to rouse her. She would turn over and go back to sleep and I would try to wake her again. After a few attempts, she would finally open her eyes and pick up her tea. 'Ugh,' she'd say in disgust, 'It's cold'. I would trudge back downstairs to get another and by the time I got up to her bedside she'd be fast asleep again.

Waking my mother was like waking the dead, and I hated the job, but not waking her was worse. I tried it once and she went ballistic, so the next morning I redoubled my efforts.

Every day after she finished work, my mum walked for ten minutes to Sainsbury's to do the shopping. She then trudged the fifteen minutes home, weighted down by a carrier bag in each hand. She was barely through the door before the three of us pounced on the bags of shopping, carrying them off to the kitchen and divesting them of crisps, fruit and yoghurts, devouring it all and then waiting for Mum to cook the dinner. She held on to one bag. 'There's nothing in there for you.'

We knew exactly what was in there and who it was for, even if we never saw the bottles. Somehow, she concealed them, and we only ever witnessed one glass of alcohol at a time, in her hand. It was as though she had a magic tap in the sky.

As we fought over packets of crisps in the

kitchen, Mum was still in the hallway shrieking, 'Get off me! Get off me!' We eyed each other and giggled. Bruiser played this game every day. He waited eagerly for Mum to get in from work then pinned her against the wall and humped her leg desperately, as if she was his long-lost mate. We went back to the hallway to watch the amorous dog show, which was always funny although Mum's irritation spoilt it a bit.

It was a bleary day in Boscombe. The town centre was filled with vagabonds. Hooligans, Dad would have said. The homeless, the jobless, the hungry, the addicted. Mum had come out of the shop laden with bags and was about to embark on her journey home. I was nearby, although she hadn't yet seen me. I had come to surprise her by helping her carry the bags home. But somebody else was lying in wait too, and he got to her first.

My father. She glanced up at him wearily. She looked as if she knew what was coming and wasn't surprised by it, but I was shocked at the suddenness of his public, verbal abuse. He was screaming at my Mum, ranting at the top of his voice. 'Fucking whore! Fucking filthy stinking prostitute! That's right, fucking walk off, you fucking bitch!'

She had no choice but to walk off, slowly, hampered by the weight of the shopping. She was wearing her blue nurse's uniform, and everyone in the street was staring at the spectacle, the looming, loony old man shouting and swearing, the nurse walking away from him with her head down, tears streaming down her face so she could hardly see where she was going.

Neither of them saw me. 'Shit,' I thought. 'I wonder how often this happens.' I felt sure my mum wouldn't like to know that I had witnessed it, so I pretended that I hadn't. I took a different route home and arrived after her, which meant that I missed the rituals of the bag opening and the dog humping. That weekend, she sent us off for our visit to Dad as usual. I had still never heard her utter a single word of criticism of her ex-husband.

25
Kissing

Since Dad was out of the picture at home, Jane and I could go to Pokesdown Youth Club whenever we wanted. It was there I met my first boyfriend, Martin. He was as spotty as me and as inexperienced a kisser, so my passion soon waned. One evening he turned up at the youth club in a neck brace, looking even more unprepossessing than usual. The kiss he gave me at the end of that evening was to my mind a goodbye-forever kiss but I didn't bother to tell the poor boy, just ignored him studiously until he eventually grasped the point.

Martin was the first in a series of brief attachments that I formed at Pokesdown Youth Club. I soon became more experienced at kissing and progressed to mild, and then heavy, petting. There was no chance of my mother finding out what I was up to, because the youth club leaders had a duty of confidentiality to the club members. Which meant that my behaviour and morals declined undetected, under the shady umbrella of the Dorset Youth Service.

When we realised that Mum had not loosened the reins but let go of them entirely, my sister and I ventured to the 896 Club, the place that had intrigued us from the vantage point of our bedroom window over the old shop. It was also run by the Youth Service, and to our delight was even seedier than we had imagined. Down in that basement you could buy single cigarettes for 5p each, and chip butties made with white bread and real butter for 25p. It was heaven for juvenile delinquents.

The people Debbie and I hung around with out of school were all a few years older than us, and a lot of them lived together, in houses that had been divided into bedsitting rooms. One of these was situated above a dry-cleaning business in Southbourne. The first time I visited that building was with Debbie, to see her friend Jon, a gangling curly-haired boy/man. Jon was cheerful, but thin and unkempt. He wore the same jeans and a battered nylon jumper, which was blue or perhaps grey, every single time I ever met him. I don't believe he owned any other clothes.

The single room that Jon lived in was bare, poorly decorated but reasonably clean. I was not shocked by his lack of possessions, which was normal for the sort of people I was mixing with (as it was for myself). What did make an impression on me was the cigarette he shared with us. He rolled it carefully, using a patchwork of Rizla papers and tobacco from a proper cigarette (he discarded the filter). He then added a third material, a sticky brown nugget which he melted using a lighter, and then crumbled into the line of tobacco. He folded up the paper carefully, lit his creation, and inhaled deeply. After a few deep drags he passed it to Debbie, who did the same, then passed it on to me.

Debbie had told me what to expect before we arrived at Jon's bedsit. She had smoked dope with him on previous occasions, and we had gone there with the intent to do so today. I was still dressed in my grammar school uniform, and was well aware that smoking dope was one step further into trouble than I had ventured before. I also knew that it was illegal, but so was under-age drinking and that had become routine for me by this point.

I toked on the joint (the language that came with the new territory rather appealed to me) and I rapidly experienced the effects. I didn't find it pleasant. I felt a sense of disconnection from reality, followed by paranoia. In fact, the best part of the whole thing was when Debbie and I finally left the dingy environment and I gradually regained my senses out in the open air.

I didn't let the negative experience put me off. I persisted, as I had done with smoking cigarettes, until I acquired a taste for cannabis too. After all, it was a cheap method of intoxication, free in fact because I never bought any of my own. I wouldn't have known where to get hold of it, even if I had any money. I just joined in whenever a joint was passed around, which seemed to be most of the time.

I was fourteen years old. I had left Roedean only a year earlier but it already felt like a world away, in both time and space.

I spent a lot of time with Debbie, both in and out of school. I often went to her home because it was warm and comfortable and her mother was so welcoming. When my father had lived with us, Debbie was not allowed to visit our house. He knew nothing about her but had disliked her on sight, and even now that he no longer lived with us he still ranted about her. He said she was leading me into bad ways, an accusation that for once was well founded, although I had no idea how he knew.

Debbie was my soulmate, at that time. She was as troubled as I was, although I couldn't work out why. Nobody in her family seemed to be a bully or an alcoholic. Her house was full of love. She even got pocket money, which was the holy grail as far as I was concerned. But for whatever reason, Debbie was a rebel, and we spent hours together talking, listening, smoking and drinking.

Without Debbie's companionship I would have been desperately lonely. I need friends. My sister Jane was different. She found it easier to make friends than I did but seemed to need them much less. She was braver and bolder than me. I longed to be more like her, but it was hopeless. I was a quivering wreck, a bag of nerves, in every situation.

I drank regularly, but alcohol never became an integral part of my life. I didn't need to drink much at all to get tipsy, but I was wary of alcohol. I knew what it could do to a person. It could take the essence of them and strip it away, reducing them to a shell, a parody of their previous selves. And, worse perhaps, the victims, the addicts, never realised it was happening. Well, it wasn't going to happen to me. I was never going to disappear into the ether, as my mother had.

26
Cannabis

I quickly slipped into the druggie way of life. I both liked and loathed being stoned. I became paranoid, scared and panicky the first time I smoked cannabis and every time I smoked it from then on. That should have been enough to put me off. But I rapidly became addicted, so smoking dope was also a relief and a release. At the time the science said that it was impossible to become addicted to cannabis but I knew this to be untrue, because I recognised the tug of addiction in myself from the start.

Smoking dope was a sociable pastime as there were always plenty of people willing to share a joint. Because it tended to be smoked in dark, dingy environments with a group of people sitting together sharing the joints but barely talking, the essence of it suited me. My shyness was easily hidden in these groups. I had the solace of company, which I craved, but without the pressure of having to be sociable, which I never understood how to achieve.

I never took any harder drugs, but then I never needed to. The effects I felt from dope alone were strong enough and frightening enough to warn me off anything else, which was lucky, because most of the older boys (and girls) who Debbie and I smoked with gradually started to try harder drugs, and a lot of them got into serious trouble as a result.

Maybe it was because of all the dope that my teenage years have blurred together in my memory. I was fourteen forever, then finally fifteen… Time passed excruciatingly slowly. I had a series of boyfriends, because boyfriends made me feel normal and wanted. I did not do much with them at first. I progressed from my first boyfriend and the bad kissing experience, which was wet and not much more, to a more experienced boy who knew how to kiss. This led to petting, and in turn to heavy petting.

The relationships never lasted long. I never wanted to take them to what the boys considered was the natural conclusion. I was well aware of the dangers of pregnancy, and I made sure to avoid it. I was grateful to my mother's magazines for this. She still bought Woman and Woman's Own every week, and from them I gleaned information about sex. I also learned about dieting although I never needed to follow any diets. I ate like a horse but remained as naturally thin as a whippet, due to my nervous tendencies and high levels of activity.

I worked hard as a teenager, taking various part-time jobs for pocket money. My first was in a bakery. I was still only thirteen when I got this job, but I told my new boss that I was fifteen. I worked there in the summer holidays and earned good money, £2.50 an hour. My sister Jane met me from work at the end of the day, when I was allowed to take home the bread and cakes that hadn't been sold. She polished off the best of them before we reached home.

In September, Keith, who ran the bakery, asked me to stay on as a Saturday worker. 'You'll meet our other Saturday girl, Jenny,' he told me. She goes to your school. In fact, she might be in your class. She's sixteen.'

I was horrified. I dreaded meeting Jenny but when the time came, my way with words – the fact that I rarely spoke any – worked to my advantage. By questioning me and answering her own questions, Jenny decided that I must be in the year below her at school, which must have been why our paths hadn't crossed before. She asked me what O levels I was taking, and laughed when I said I couldn't remember (the truth was that I hadn't started the O level syllabus yet). When Jenny saw me in the corridor at school and I was sure she would twig that I was with girls who were three years younger than she was, the penny still didn't drop. I continued my under-age work at the bakery unexposed.

School ticked along in a mostly unsatisfactory way but without any great upheavals. Debbie was not so lucky. She fell behind with her academic work, and because her attendance was low as well, she was asked to leave. She moved to a nearby comprehensive and quickly made new friends there, although we still saw each other in the pub in the evenings.

27
Alcohol

My father's living conditions deteriorated over the next few years. His first flat was decent enough, a garden flat with two or three rooms. But if my mother had little idea of housekeeping, he had none at all, and the place soon became filthy. He got behind with his rent. He lived on benefits and the flat was too expensive to be covered by Housing Benefit, but he secured his tenancy by offering to top up the payments from his own funds. He gave the landlady, a kindly person, his benefits book as security and told her that every week she was to accompany him to the Post Office where he would hand her £20.

What actually happened was very different. Every week Dad gambled every penny, asked for his benefits book back to cash the payments himself, railed against his landlady for taking it in the first place... Within a few months he had the poor woman going in circles, distressed beyond belief, not knowing whether or when she would be paid. He became verbally abusive towards her, and consequently found himself out on his ear. Homeless.

This began a downward spiral, as he moved from one shabby bedsitting room to another. Things would usually begin well because at the outset of each tenancy he charmed his landladies with his cutglass accent and dulcet tones. But they all ended up less than entranced with his lack of personal hygiene, his chain smoking and, particularly, the pisspot he kept under the bed in case he got caught short in the middle of the night.

None of my elder sisters or brother ever visited Dad, or us. We heard from them only occasionally. Mandy was still abroad, and Belita was busy working in the jewellery business her partner was building up. As time went on, even we youngest three only saw our father occasionally, and then only out of guilt; his birthday, Father's Day. My mother had finally given up forcing us to visit him weekly after an unsavoury episode when, during a lull in warfare, she went to see him herself. We don't know what happened on this visit, but it evidently persuaded her that he was not a healthy influence on anybody, including his own children.

My father occasionally attempted to keep up appearances. Whenever he had a decent win, he bundled up all his clothes, underwear and all, and took them to the dry cleaner. However, as time went on, the winning streaks became few and far between and he cleaned up less often. The Savile Row suits, once his pride and joy, were now thirty years old and hung off his emaciated frame, tragically stained with episodes of incontinence.

I found this deterioration painful to witness. My father was a sorrowful figure and I still felt the odd pang of affection for him. But I could see few redeeming characteristics in him and although I would have liked to help in some way, I knew I was powerless to do so. He was a hopeless case.

Meanwhile, I had an active life of my own. I was never part of a gang or a group of close friends but I had Debbie and I was on the fringes of a group who met regularly in the local pub in the evenings. The landlord was relaxed about the licensing laws, which was fortunate as I was still only fifteen when I started to hang out there.

I continued working my way through a series of boyfriends, engaging in behaviour that my mother, however distant she had become, would definitely not have approved of. Lucky, then, that she never asked. We were all allowed to go our own way, and the unspoken agreement was that we would not comment on our mother's way of life if she did not interfere with ours.

She was drinking a lot. I don't know when she went from a glass or two to unwind at the end of a hard day to full-blown, constant drunkenness but it looked like it was going to be a one-way journey. Every day ended with Mum, paralytic, perilously ascending the stairs to her bed. Often, Jane and I had to half-push, half-carry her up.

By now we knew she kept her booze in the cupboard under the kitchen sink. Lager, cider or wine, depending on how much money she had to spare. One day Jane suggested pouring Mum's stash away into the sink. We looked at each other, weighed up the consequences, and decided it wasn't worth it. She would be angry and, because Mum's anger was so rare, it was more to be feared. And anyway, pouring her stash away wouldn't change anything.

When Mum found out that my sister and I smoked, she was not happy. Jane was fourteen, I was thirteen. Mum was grumpy and sulky with us, like a child annoyed with its parents. But she quickly decided that it was better that she knew what was going on and because there was no point in us hiding it now, she announced that we could smoke at home.

We smoked at home for a week or so, feeling a bit odd about it. One evening my mother, wobbly with drink, spotted Jane coming down the stairs with a lit cigarette and started to yell at her. 'What on earth do you think you're doing with that cigarette?' she shouted.

'But Mum,' my sister wailed, 'You said I could!' Clearly this was a reality check for my mother, who looked comically surprised. She had completely forgotten, but she must have known she was drunk and incapable of rational argument. She gathered her dignity, asked vaguely, 'Oh, did I?' and then drifted off to her usual position in front of the television to drown her confusion. Jane pulled a face at me behind Mum's back.

I wasn't often at home in the evenings, but Jane and Stephen were hardly there at all. I would push my armchair a foot or two from the television so that I could see it, still refusing to wear my glasses even at home. Mum had moved to the chair in the corner, the one that Dad used to occupy. I had seen him there for so long that I imagined I could see him still, deep in thought, the familiar cylinder of ash collecting on the tip of his fag. 'Ash, Dad! Ash!'

Now that I could smoke at home, my mother often gave me cigarettes herself, later in the evening when she was properly tipsy. Otherwise, when Jane and I were desperate, we had fertile pickings in the ashtrays because Mum left very long stubs. Like Dad, she never inhaled her smoke.

I always inhaled. It was the thing I liked most about smoking cigarettes; the harsh, painful, satisfying catch in my throat as I pulled the smoke into my lungs. Smoking Mum's leftover ends was the thing I liked least about it, but I had no choice because by now I was well and truly addicted to nicotine. Mum bum-sucked her fags. Jane and I learned this lovely word at the pub. It meant the filters were wet, soaked with her spit, and the next morning they were cold and soggy. Mum did not know the right way to smoke a cigarette at all.

She occasionally offered me a drink of lager or cider but although I accepted the cigarettes, I refused the alcohol. My silent rebellion against my circumstances was that I would never accept a drink from my mother.

I operated double standards, because I was perfectly happy to drink in the pub. There, I scrounged half pints of lager and blackcurrant or lager and lime. They cost about 50p, and it only took two or three for me to become comfortably pissed. I was careful not to drink so much that I lost control.

Except on the memorable day when I teamed up with an older girl, Laura. I knew her from Pokesdown Youth club. She was seventeen, and lived with her alcoholic father. She was a friendly, kind sort of girl and I happily accepted her invitation to her flat, where we drank half a bottle of her Dad's gin, neat, between us. Laura was used to spirits but I ended up extremely unwell. I was vomiting heavily by the time someone found Jane and brought her Laura's place to smuggle me home.

I never drank spirits again and became more wary of all alcohol. But I didn't associate smoking dope with my mother's addiction, so I indulged more and more frequently. Cannabis was everywhere I went. It would affect my life as much as if I had fallen prey to cocaine or heroin, as several of my contemporaries did.

I was a mess. I was horrendously shy, and was developing a phobia about blushing that made me feel extremely foolish. I had panic attacks in case I blushed and, together, the blushing and panic attacks became incapacitating. I felt anxious and awkward around people, though I still sought out company because I could not bear to be alone. But I still blundered on with my foolish ways, not knowing where I could turn for help. I didn't even know that asking for help was an option.

28
Oxbridge

At school I kept my head down, becoming so quiet as to be almost inconspicuous. I had a few friends in my year group, other girls who had started to rebel by smoking behind the bike sheds. I didn't know them as well as I knew Debbie and I rarely saw them out of school once she had left. I was often alone in school and I was absent a great deal, either turning up late or taking whole days off. My attendance rate at that time was about fifty per cent.

It had been a long time since I excelled at my schoolwork but I didn't fall too far behind. I did my homework, between or during lessons, and when there were tests or exams, I revised enough to make sure I passed. I had a good short-term memory and could swot up enough to pass any exam although the minute it was over, I forgot everything I had learned. In those days at the grammar school, we had no coursework to worry about. Everything was assessed by exams, which suited me fine.

I still loved English, and my English teacher, who was also my form teacher, recognised that I was more attentive in her classes than the others. She approached me one day as I was reading at my desk.

'Louise?'

I looked up. 'Yes, Miss Longhurst?'

'I think you have a chance of taking the Oxbridge exam. Have you read a book called Emma by Jane Austen?'

'No, Miss Longhurst.'

'Well, you should read it. Let me know how you

get on.'

This episode prompted mixed feelings. On the one hand, it was a boost to my confidence that someone still recognised my academic potential. I had been marked out as a definite Oxbridge candidate when I was at Roedean.

However, by now I had changed so much that I knew I was a world away from getting into one of these universities. There would be an interview, which I knew I would fail. By this time, I could hardly get a word out in public, and in any formal situation I literally quaked with fear. I knew that even if I really pulled myself together and began to study properly, I was not Oxbridge material. In any case, Miss Longhurst never broached the subject again.

The teachers had no idea about me. They didn't know that I smoked dope out of school or about my boyfriends. They could never have envisaged the depths of poverty and misery in my home. And I only had myself to blame for their lack of interest, because I had been uncooperative and surly at school for so long. The only time the teaching staff showed any sympathy for my situation was when the news of my parents' divorce filtered through, which was bizarre because the divorce was the best thing that had happened in my family for a long time.

The long slide of my marks at school and my complete lack of enthusiasm for education continued unheeded. I was an impossible child to engage with and there were plenty of others at BSG more deserving of attention. I was just plain miserable, and with the best of intentions no teacher could have reached me.

My home life really was a shambles. The house was filthy. Bruiser the Alsatian and our new cat, Minx, left hairs and dirt everywhere and nobody cleaned it up. At least the cat had taken some of Bruiser's attention away from my mother. We got him as a kitten, free from an advert in the local paper. Minx was only six weeks old when he came to live with us, and he missed his mother. He curled up with Bruiser in the dog's basket and tried to breastfeed from him, and the sweet, mad Alsatian let him try.

Cigarettes and their stink in the house, dog shit in the garden, buried in the waist-high grass. Three teenage kids to deal with. Dust and debris all around. Full-time work at the hospital but never enough money to go around. It was all too much for my poor mother. She was averse to housework anyway, and the rest of us had no idea where to start. Jane and I did operate the washing machine occasionally, washing and drying our own school uniforms when it became unavoidable. We hardly ever had anything new, not even shoes.

We were all helpless in practical matters. I had no idea, for example, that other people decorated their homes. My experience was that you moved into a home and lived there, and during the time you were there you did as little as possible in the way of maintenance or cleaning or any other sort of home-based activity. We never took a family holiday either. The last one we ever had was when we went to Israel.

We knew how hard life was for my mother, although she never complained. We hated to see her drunk but we accepted that alcohol was a necessary part of her life. Once when Stephen wanted a computer, the early BBC version, he asked Mum for it, and somehow she found the money. She was softly spoken, civilised, an angel. She never said a bad word against anybody. Literally, not ever.

But when Mum was drunk, she was a different person. She slurred and slopped around, becoming sentimental and tedious. She would stare down at her hands, fan out her fingers. 'See this ring? Your father gave it to me. See this one here? Mandy gave me that one.' There were tears in her eyes. 'See this ring on this finger? This is the one that was in the pawn shop for so long that Mandy bought back for me.' Still gazing down at her hands, she would begin again, 'See this ring? Your father gave it to me...'

At the dinner table in the evenings, nobody attempted conversation. Mum didn't eat with us. She laid our plates on the table, we guzzled our food and then we retreated to our rooms. There were no family outings, no celebrations on special occasions. No sense of togetherness. I grew up in a fragmented household, and my natural shyness became incapacitating. I was a shell of a person.

29
Spots

In some ways, I was living a teenager's dream. My mother's laissez faire policy meant that I could, and did, leave the house and return to it whenever I chose. I made the most of this freedom, although that often involved walking home alone and terrified in the early hours of the morning.

Mum didn't ask about my love life. I could snog, or more, whoever I wanted, providing they wanted to snog me back. Someone always did. I looked older than my age, I was slim with long fair hair, and I was accommodating. I still held back from anything more than heavy petting. I was still reading my mother's women's magazines. I knew all about pregnancy and I intended to avoid it at all costs.

I was vain. I had little in the way of raw material to carve out any sort of style, but I was interested in how I looked and what I wore. I owned a green sweatshirt, a white sweatshirt and one pair of jeans. I somehow acquired a ra-ra skirt, which was also white and which, when combined with the sweatshirt pulled down sufficiently tightly to cover the first ruffle of the skirt, looked reasonably cool. At least, I thought so.

My spots were an obsession. I squeezed them, poked them and stared at them for hours on end. My best friend was a spot concealer from Boots, which I smeared on top of the spots so that the redness was covered by a greasy brown stain.

When she was sixteen, Jane started work full-time, and moved into a flat. I missed her. But I soon moved on, when I went out for the first time with the gorgeous eighteen-year-old cockney lad whose parents owned a shop down the road. I thought all my dreams had come true. Olly took me to a nightclub. He never stopped talking, but I had no idea what he was on about because the music was so loud that I couldn't hear a word he was saying. He didn't seem to mind when I didn't speak back.

We walked home at three in the morning, and halfway up my road he pulled me under the awning of the cigarette shop on the corner. We sat on the pavement and entwined our bodies. So far, so familiar. But then to my amazement, Olly turned out to have a kind of sexual Tourette's. His efforts at caressing me were accompanied with an unexpected and non-stop monologue of filthy commentary. I found it off-putting. I had realised by now that he was talkative, but this was ridiculous.

When Olly eventually calmed down, we walked home in silence. He had finally shut up. We became aware there were lights flashing in the air and as we rounded the corner we saw they were blue. The fire engine was parked outside my house. My mother had recently acquired a car, and it was blazing in the street. The firemen were extinguishing the flames. Most of the street was out gawping. Except, I realised, my mother and brother.

I panicked. Where were they? I ran upstairs shouting at the top of my voice, 'Mum! Steve! MUM!' My throat closed, I was choking with fear. There was no reply. They must have been in the car, they had both burned to death. I was screaming as I pushed open Mum's bedroom door. She was fast asleep, head to one side, her face squashed against the pillow. Flat out. In Stephen's room, when I finally got access (he had rigged up a complicated system to lock his door from inside) it was the same story. Both had slept like babies throughout all the commotion.

The firemen said that the car had an electrical fault. Olly and I didn't go out together again, by mutual consent.

I have tried hard to come up with a chronological account of my teenage years but a lot of it eludes me. A lot of it eluded me even then, since I was largely confused, stoned and myopic.

I do know that I didn't always appreciate the freedom my mother accorded me. One day I insisted she should come to the parents' evening at school. Perhaps I was trying to regain a grip on my education.

But the outing made both of us miserable. My mother, bolstered by Dutch courage, talked to the teachers alone as I skulked unhappily in the car, refusing to come into the school until forced to do so by one of my teachers, who made her way to the car park, tapped on the car window and, when I reluctantly wound it down, insisted that I follow her inside. Then I lurked sulkily in the hall behind my mother, bright red with embarrassment and unable to concentrate on what was being said.

Mum turned to me sharply as we walked to the car park together. 'Now, you don't want to do that again, do you?' she snapped.

'No,' I muttered back. But I did. I wanted to do it properly, with my head held high, able to converse with my teachers, supported by a caring and sober mother.

When I was fifteen, I got a part-time job as a waitress in a pizza restaurant. I worked with Gemma and Pippa, who were sixteen and seventeen and both completely in awe of the owner, Ali. Ali was unpredictable, prone to outbursts of anger. I couldn't have cared less, and I paid him no attention at all. The other girls found it hard to believe how insouciant I was and often told me I was brave.

I didn't feel I deserved their admiration and respect. I wasn't scared of Ali simply because I knew that he couldn't hurt me and that I could walk out of the job any time I liked and find a similar one elsewhere. I had been helpless against the anger of my father, and this made me determined never to live in fear of anybody else.

In the school holidays I often took waitressing or chambermaid jobs in hotels. One of these, Oak Hall in Boscombe, was close to the Shelley Museum. When I learned that Percy Bysshe Shelley once lived near here, something chimed in me. A distant memory of a handsome young teacher and his French wife at Durlston Court, a couple nobody met except me. But I didn't believe in ghosts, I wouldn't believe in ghosts. I dismissed the thought.

Mum got an extra job. She called it moonlighting, and it was against the terms of her contract of employment. In addition to her full-time work at the hospital, she now worked at a nursing home all night on Thursdays, Fridays and Saturdays nights.

Jane and I took turns going to work with Mum. We were employed as care assistants, but the way we saw it we were protecting Mum from herself. Each week I sat beside her in the car, absolutely terrified, as she drove to work. She had taken to drinking vodka, Jane said because she thought it couldn't be smelled on her breath. She didn't usually drink spirits, so each week she would be absolutely rolling drunk before we arrived at the nursing home.

She drove at less than twenty miles an hour,

holding up all the traffic behind. I found it excruciating. 'The car knows where to go' she slurred. 'I don't know the way at all, but my car is very clever. It will get us there.'

I heard the siren before I saw the flashing blue lights. The police car was right behind us. Mum swore, stared at the road ahead, and kept crawling along. This is it, I thought. She is going to be in massive trouble for this. I braced myself. But the car passed us, its lights disappearing off into the darkness ahead.

The proprietor of the nursing home would brief Mum on the condition of the patients and count out our pay for the evening. I would hold my breath. Surely, surely this man couldn't be unaware of how completely drunk my mother was. She'd be slurring her words, swaying on her feet. But he was seemingly oblivious.

I hated my Saturday nights at the nursing home. It smelled awful. I peeled potatoes and Mum saw to the patients, then we watched television and at about eleven we bedded down for the night. We slept on piles of cushions laid on the floor. The smell was worse down there, close to the carpet. I'd think about how lucky Mum was that I was there to keep an eye on her as I drifted off to sleep. Occasionally I was woken by Mum padding around, going to check on patients, but she never asked me to help. One night a patient died but I was completely unaware of it until morning. I'd just vaguely noted that Mum had been more active than usual during the night.

It never occurred to me that I was the lucky one. I had a sinecure of a job. I got a lift to work, where I peeled some potatoes, watched some TV then slept soundly through the night. My mother, working for sixty

148

hours on the trot, somehow remained conscious and capable, caring for her patients through the days and the hours of darkness. And she managed all this regardless of her terrible ailment. Despite the curse of alcoholism, my mother was a fine nurse.

31
Sweet Sixteen

My birthday always fell during the half-term holiday
from school. The day I turned sixteen, I was in bed with
a stomach-ache. Mum usually ignored our teenage
maladies, but this time, after I began to cry with the
discomfort, she called the GP. When he arrived, he
pressed my stomach with his cold hands, watching me
carefully for a reaction.

'Does this hurt? And this?'

'Yes. Ow'.

His expression was sceptical. He was clearly
irritated at being called out to attend a teenager.

'How old are you, Louise?'

'Sixteen. Today'.

'Ah. Have you got a stomach-ache because you
were out drinking with your friends last night? If you
tell me, I won't tell your mother.'

I would have laughed if my stomach didn't hurt
so much. This man really had no idea of the dynamics in
our household. I looked at him wearily, making sure that
I got eye contact, that he was listening properly.

'I do drink' I said. There was no shame in my
admission. 'But I was not drinking last night'.

The doctor was taken aback. He'd thought he
had me sussed, a sweet sixteen who was ill after her first
drink. Now he saw something different in my eyes and
he believed me. He admitted me to hospital with
suspected appendicitis.

At the hospital things moved fast, and it was still the
same day when I woke up from the anaesthetic, feeling
sick. I managed to focus on a young, good-looking

doctor at my bedside. 'We took your appendix out just before it ruptured. It had pus on the outside,' he informed me. He held out a jar towards me. 'Would you like to see it?'

'No!' I glared at him as if he was mad and he drifted away, still clutching his jar.

I went home the next day. I didn't like the hospital. I couldn't sleep and there was nothing to do there. Smoking was no consolation because cigarettes didn't taste nice at all in that sterile atmosphere. My mother was the Sister in the hospital's Outpatients Department, and promised to look after me at home, so they let me out early.

But when I arrived home, for the first time in my life I became angry with my mother. The hospital was a horrid uncomfortable place but it had been spotlessly clean. My home, by contrast, was as filthy as usual and it disappointed me. I don't know why I thought things would have changed in the short time I had been away, but I did. I raged about it the dirt and the chaos, and my mother cried.

We didn't really do presents in our family. We didn't have the means. It was totally unexpected, then, when Mum took me to the optician and got me fitted for contact lenses as a sixteenth birthday present. They cost £100, a staggering amount of money. I was very grateful. I had never got used to wearing my glasses and consequently when the optician puts the lenses into my eyes it was a complete revelation. I could see!

But when I got home, things did not progress smoothly. I could not pluck up the courage to insert the lenses myself. I spent ages in front of the bathroom mirror, lens on the end of my finger, trying to poke myself in the eye, but I couldn't do it. I tried every day for a week, getting increasingly upset. My mother cornered me one day and shouted at me fiercely, 'I spent one hundred pounds on those lenses and you're not wearing them!'

Mum was never angry. I retreated to the bathroom, put the lens on the end of my finger once again. Stared at it. Braced myself. Gathered my courage. It took forever, but finally I stabbed myself in the eye. It was in!

I shouted downstairs to my mother, 'I've done it! I've done it! Mum! I've done it!'

Hang on a minute. Oh bugger. Now I had to do the other one...

32
Bedsit Land

I left home after my O level exams, most of which I passed without fuss and without distinction. I had spent four years at Bournemouth School for Girls just getting by, academically. I attended the school's Founders Day Service in July of 1985. All the other girls arrived with their parents, wearing outfits specially bought for the occasion; little suits with little hats and little shoes. It was like watching a fashion parade as my peers climbed onto the stage one by one, collected their certificates and walked off to the sound of applause.

Founders Day was always held in the big hall in the Bournemouth Winter Gardens. I sat alone in the hall, wearing denim jeans. I had forgotten that everyone got dressed up for this occasion and I was embarrassed, although I had no other clothes to wear in any case. I didn't fully understand the magnitude of what I was doing, how far I had deviated from the norm. It was only when I heard the collective 'Oh' of shock from thousands of parents and students as I mounted the stage to collect my certificate that I realised I must have been the first person in the history of Bournemouth School for Girls to wear jeans to collect her certificates on Founders Day.

On my way out, I saw Debbie's little sister Sarah, who was a couple of years below me at school. I tried to avoid her gaze. Sarah was sweet, but I couldn't bear to talk to anybody because I was still smarting from the humiliation.

She wouldn't let me go. 'Louise!' she called out. 'Hey! Lou!' I couldn't ignore her. She rushed over. 'I

153

can't believe you wore jeans on stage! That was so cool! I'm going to do that when it's my turn!'

I didn't bother to explain that it hadn't been deliberate.

My mother was moving to a council house in Kinson, a distant run-down suburb of Bournemouth, and I didn't want to go with her so I left home. I found a bedsit for myself and Minx the cat. Minx was my cat. I was the only member of the family he allowed to pick him up and when I did, he purred in my arms. If Stephen or our mother tried to pick him up, he hissed and spat at them. He would meet me at the top of the road after school and walk home with me along the top of the garden walls. We adored each other.

The bedsit was so close to our old house, just on the other side of our old garden wall, that Minx soon got used to his new abode. I enrolled in a local sixth form college to take my A levels, and claimed Social Security and Housing Benefit. It was a pittance but I could afford to make ends meet, so long as I didn't smoke. Which, of course, I did.

33
Louise and Dave

I was nearly seventeen when I got together with Dave.
He was nineteen, a sweet boy with a big smile. He'd had
a serious motorbike accident and his leg was pinned
together in several places, immobilised in a plaster cast.
This means that Dave was a sitting duck when I set my
sights on him.

I was well aware of my attractiveness to men.
What they liked was my hair, which was very light
brown, straight and thick, hanging down to my waist.
What men didn't notice, or mind about, was my lack of
conversation. In fact I think some of them preferred it,
because they were happy to talk for as long as I was
happy to listen.

I never had a head for drink. Half a lager and
blackcurrant and I was wobbly. Two halves and I was
drunk. In the pub most evenings, bolstered by Dutch
courage, I slid myself into the booth next to Dave. I
smiled shyly at him and melted when he smiled back,
that slow smile of his. He told me about his accident,
how it made him feel to be so ill, helpless, how he hated
being off work for so long. I nodded carefully,
sympathetically.

Soon I knew all about Dave. Dave saw in me
whatever it was he wanted to see, and we got together as
I had hoped. I was timetabled for only eighteen hours of
study a week at the college, and I didn't see the need to
be there for more than half of that time, so I had a lot of
free hours to spend with my new boyfriend. For months
we were glued at the hip.

Things became serious quickly. Dave's bedsit was not

155

as grotty as mine, so we spent most of our time there. I didn't like the poster of Kate Bush on his wall. I was jealous of her. But sensibly, I kept that to myself.

I moved from my bedsit to a shared flat, but my flatmate turned out to be a heroin addict, so I moved again. I moved five times during my first year at college. Eventually, Dave and I got a flat together. This became our home for the next three years.

Being with Dave was like being married. We were devoted to one another, we did everything together and we never argued. I studied for my A levels and, when he finally recovered from his operation, he worked as a glazier. We shopped at Sainsbury's once a week and we watched a carefully curated schedule of TV programmes in the evenings.

We went out with Dave's friends occasionally. I didn't really like them, for the same reason that I didn't like Kate Bush. I was very insecure and this made me jealous. But again, I kept it all to myself. I went with Dave and his friends to watch Iron Maiden at Wembley. I went to Glastonbury Festival with them. I had no real taste for rock music. I preferred music with lyrics, words I could hear and understand. But I never said so.

All I wanted was to be with Dave and I persevered at the task until our identities merged. We were Dave and Louise now. Louise and Dave. There was no longer a 'me', only an 'us', and in that new identity I found a little peace at last.

34
Christmas

Dave came from a solidly middle-class family. His mother Muriel and her sisters were midwives and his dad Doug was a postman. All of them had a strong work ethic and lived organised, structured, moral existences. It was, as far as I could tell, an ideal family.

Every week, Dave, his sister Karen and I gathered at Muriel and Doug's for Sunday lunch and a mutual dissection of our lives. They were strange meals compared to what I was used to at home; quiet, discursive, civilised.

When it was time to say grace before the meal I didn't join in because I was conflicted about religion, but Muriel liked me and turned a blind eye to this failing, because I was a nice girl from a good family. She said this aloud one day and I choked on my roast chicken. I made a mental note that she must never, ever be allowed to meet my mother or visit my family home.

Dave's family were all Christians, except Dave. His mother hoped he would return to the flock one day. Christmas was the best time to be a part of his family, in my opinion. Doug had been a widower when he met Muriel and already had two daughters, who were equally impeccably presented and behaved. They would arrive with their families, adding to the atmosphere.

Their Christmas rituals were well-established, and bestowed a sense of belonging even on me, the newest and most tentative member of the family. I was drilled on the procedure. We all wrote a list of presents we might like, well in advance of the day, and distributed it to the family. Then each person chose a present from the list, ticked it off and passed the list on.

I couldn't remember the last time anyone in my own family had given me a Christmas gift and I struggled to decide what to put on my list. Dave's mum was much better at this. She selected a set of copper-bottomed saucepans and orchestrated the process so that somebody was designated to collect the cash contributions and buy the exact ones she had chosen. I was fascinated. I had no idea that this was how families were supposed to function.

Muriel received her saucepans in advance so she could use them on Christmas Day. They were hung carefully above the range, taking pride of place in her neat and tidy kitchen, heart of a loving family home.

I tried to compare all these preparations with Christmas at my home. We did celebrate Christmas, even when my father was going through his Jewish phase. We always ate a turkey meal, with rice as well as potatoes because this was a 'Gillett family tradition'. The alcohol flowed, and the inflammatory Val Doonican was on the telly. When his crooning face appeared, Mum would remind us all that she went out with him back in the day, though we couldn't have forgotten this fact if we'd tried.

Every year, a few weeks before Christmas, strings of cards would suddenly appear in the lounge and dining room, scores of them. This never failed to surprise me as I had no idea that we had so many friends. Or any, in fact. I didn't recognise the names on the cards, but the fact that they were there made me feel comforted that these people cared about our family.

In fact, the Christmas cards were the one thing about our family that made me feel pleased, proud and relieved, until the day Jane pointed out that the cards didn't arrive in the post. They were relics from previous years that my mother kept, hanging up the same cards every year. Jane said I was an idiot for not realising this myself, and I readily agreed with her.

Christmas Day at Dave's house was a revelation. We sat comfortably and opened our presents in turn. It was a lesson on elegant living. One by one each person slowly opened a gift, exclaimed politely and thanked the giver. When it was my turn I blushed chartreuse with all the eyes on me. I slowly opened my first gift. It was from Dave. He had given me a green coat. What I really wanted was a red coat. I exclaimed politely and thanked him.

I didn't really want to be with Dave's lovely family. I wanted to be back at Wolverton Road with my own stupid family, eating dinner that had been cooked by my own mother, drunk or not. Smoking fags with my laughing, teasing siblings. Not a present in sight. Watching Val Doonican on the TV as our stupid, nervous, adorable Alsatian tried to breastfeed the cat. Those days were gone.

I put my head down, blushed, stayed quiet.

35
University

Sixth form college was murder. In the first year, I smoked a lot of dope. I don't know whether it was connected, but the blushing became overpowering. A lot of my time and thoughts were taken up with worries about when a blush would start and what I would be able to do about it. By putting all this effort into the problem, I had developed it to the point where it became rather alarming, probably as alarming to the people who witnessed it as it was to me. I was like a human chameleon. I could do the full colour range from palest rose to deepest purple, and if it was not so utterly out of my control and so misery-making it would have been an impressive achievement.

I hardly attended my classes, and I was surprised to get through my end of year exams. I went to Glastonbury with Dave and his friends to celebrate. There, I took less drugs than anybody else but got more mentally disturbed than all of them. After two days of paranoia, mud-caked and demoralised, I begged Dave to take me home.

A few months later, we gave up smoking together, both cigarettes and dope, substituting these vices with a serious ice-cream habit as we worked our way through all the flavours in Sainsbury's frozen food cabinet. I was so happy that I didn't realise how fat I had become until we visited Mandy in Rotterdam and she told me I was bursting out of my jeans and needed to do something about it. Obedient as ever, I went on a diet.

I had one friend at college, Venetia. She was sane and organised. She had never smoked anything in her life. Venetia had a steady boyfriend too. Marco was the head boy of Portchester school. Every Tuesday night we went out as a foursome, for a drink and a chat. I was never sure why Venetia chose me to be her friend, but I was so glad that she did.

It was all so safe, but I was growing unsettled. I was unused to stability. At the beginning of my second year at college Dave threw a surprise 18th birthday celebration for me at a beautiful old country pub. He arranged for Jane and her husband Tony to be waiting for me with our friends Cliff and Sue, and a cake was brought out at the end of the meal. It was all so sweet and so normal, but I felt cheated. I wanted more. I had grown up in chaos and was wired for excitement, and the life I had built with Dave was unbearably slow. I was bored, and this made me feel terribly guilty.

I gained three Bs for my A levels, which was respectable by most standards and outstanding by those of the run-down and demoralised college I attended. I accepted a place at the University of Southampton to study Law. I had wanted to be a teacher but went against my instincts for no better reason than misplaced vanity and pride at my academic ability. The principal of a local teacher training college had visited and told us we only needed to achieve two D grades at A level to get a place at his institution. This put me off. I decided I didn't want to waste my brains on teaching.

When I started university, I made a cowardly decision, ostensibly because I didn't want to leave Dave, but really because I was frightened to leave our home and knew I would have difficulties socially. I announced that I was going to avoid upheaval by commuting daily to Southampton. This way my weekends and evenings would still be spent at home with Dave.

In a way this was a good idea, except that I was growing more restless. I wanted to be friendly and outgoing and live a typically enjoyable student life but I was far too nervous for this. So, conflicted in my emotions, I drove into uni daily. I had an old car that I'd saved up for with the money from my holiday jobs, an Austin Vanden Plas. It had a sunroof, red leather seats and a walnut dashboard and little walnut tables that pulled down in the back, like the tables in an aeroplane. It cost £200 and was my pride and joy.

I did make some friends at university, and I enjoyed studying, but my nerves began to take hold more than ever. I was finding it hard coping with daily life, but at the same time I craved more excitement. I was confused.

My problem with blushing, which I'd hoped I had left behind when I stopped smoking dope, came back to haunt me. One day I was at a criminal law lecture, the first one of term. The lecturer asked if anybody present had ever been in trouble with the law. I wanted to put my hand up, tell them all about my caution for possessing cannabis when I was sixteen and spending a weekend in London with a boyfriend. I wondered what effect it would have on the straitlaced law students around me. But I was too terrified to speak. I started to change colour at the thought that I might be the centre of attention if I spoke.

I hated this, the difference between the way I was and the way I wanted to be. I found the blushing mortifying. I had no control over it and felt deeply shamed at being so noticeably embarrassed. I couldn't understand why my face betrayed me in this way. I would have given anything to be composed and articulate. Instead, I was a quivering wreck, and I despised myself for it.

Matters deteriorated. I developed a crush on one of the boys on my course. I dumped Dave in the hope of getting together with this boy. The crush became an obsession, and Jake, who may have been flattered at first, was soon freaked out by my attentiveness. The whole thing became tangled in my mind, and within two terms of starting at university I had veered completely out of control.

I had moved into a hall of residence when I split up from Dave, but soon it was the Easter holidays. I returned to Bournemouth and stayed with Jane and Tony because I had nowhere else to go. I spent days driving through the New Forest between Bournemouth and Southampton, convinced that I was on some secret mission. I had completed an essay for my politics tutor on the subject of national security and I became convinced that I was a British spy being chased by secret service agents from other countries.

I was smoking again, including dope. Tony smoked a lot of the stuff and was convinced that, if only I had enough of it, I would be as relaxed and calm as he was. I keeled over one day, blacked out in the hallway, and the cigarette I was holding burned a small, round hole in my sister's new carpet, her pride and joy. The next time I wanted to go out I couldn't find my car keys anywhere and when I looked for my car that had vanished too. My family were uninterested when I tried to enrol their help. It didn't occur to me that they might have been complicit in the disappearance of these things, for my own protection.

When the visitors began to arrive at the flat, they introduced themselves as social workers and psychiatrists. I was delighted, because I knew that this was a cover and really they were here to consult the oracle. I was the oracle, of course. It was I. And I was more than happy to hold forth to all, giving them the benefits of my wisdom. I told one eminent doctor (I knew he was eminent because of the length of his white beard) the secret of the Meaning of Life. Of course, I told him to keep it under his hat.

My mum visited too, and my sister Mandy. Mandy's sudden appearance confused me, because she had been living abroad for some time and I couldn't understand why she had come back. Mandy tutted over how thin I had become. She and Jane insisted that I stood on the bathroom scales and both exclaimed over the results.

'She's eight and a half stone!' I thought it was odd that my weight seemed to concern them more than the fact that my life was unravelling, and I felt ashamed that I had let myself get so terribly thin as to shock my sisters. Many years later, Jane told me they were jealous that I was so skinny. I had no idea of this, because for all my supposed worldly wisdom there were huge gaps in my understanding of how other people's minds worked.

I sensed that things were going wrong. The visitors I thought had come to learn from me were not on my side after all. They mocked me. I clung to Jane. Jane was the life and soul of every party. She was the light to my dark. She was everything I longed to be. Jane gave me her old clothes to wear. I was relieved, because now I could disguise myself as my sister and no-one would find me.

One evening, I was with Jane and Tony in the kitchen. It was dusk, and I had already been out to visit the moon a couple of times. I went outside again, stood on the balcony outside the flat door and talked to the moon through the clear night air. I came back in and babbled away to my sister and her husband. Suddenly, we heard the sound of gunshot, turning as one to see a bullet-sized hole in the kitchen window. Tony swore, ran outside, shouting about stupid kids with airguns. When he came back we all looked for the bullet, but it was nowhere to be found. I knew this was because it was lodged in my heart. I had been shot, and now I was dead.

The next day I read the headlines in the newspaper. A woman had put a baby into the tumble drier. I knew that it was me, and that I had hurt my dear little nephew. In fact, the reason I had not seen Thomas recently was not that I had hurt him but because Jane and Tony had sensibly kept him well away from me in my distressed state. But I would not accept their attempts at reassurance.

Things only got worse. As my fears and fantasies entwined, the delusions and blackouts became ever more constant. Eventually, everything compounded and ended in the most awful conclusion imaginable. St Ann's Hospital.

36
Convalescence

Those are my recollections of my life up to my first breakdown, that apocalyptic time when I found myself alone, mad and desperate, tumbling into chaos. Locked up in a mental hospital.

While I was in hospital Dave had finally received the compensation for his motorbike accident and he used the money to put a deposit on a two-bedroom house in Pokesdown. He waited there for me, hoping that once I recovered from my madness, I would come home.

I didn't go straight back to Dave. In all, I spent three months in St Ann's and when I was finally released, I went to stay with my mother at her council maisonette in Kinson. In the years since I'd left home, things had deteriorated. My mother still worked at the hospital and my brother Stephen still lived at home with her, but her alcoholism had the upper hand over them both. The house was dirtier than ever. Bruiser had gone because, working full-time, Mum had no time to walk him, and cooped up in the flat all day he became crazier than ever. He had to be put down.

Mum kept cats now instead. She took Minx back when I moved in with Dave, because we weren't allowed to keep him in our flat, and she acquired another cat to keep him company. Her house reeked of cats and cigarettes. On every surface, in every corner of every room, junk had accumulated. No routine existed, except that my mother went to work and somehow cooked a meal each evening. It was a mess, a jumble, a disheartening hovel.

I had been at my mother's house for a week. One day, I

had a bath, emerged from the bathroom wrapped in a towel and retreated to my small box room to get dressed. I caught a glimpse of myself in the small mirror that rested on the chest of drawers. I saw an expense of flat, white belly and was rocked by a wave of sadness which took me suddenly, so unexpectedly I felt as if it was drawing me deep underwater. I was drowning in misery and I didn't know why.

I did know that I couldn't stand living with Mum. I adored her, and I couldn't bear to see her in this condition. I had no way of helping her because I was too weak and desperate myself. So I convinced myself that I loved Dave after all, that I'd only changed when madness had crept up on me and I'd become flighty, uneasy, crazy. I had left the man I had loved for three years and chased after filaments in the air, figments of my imagination, unspoken and unspeakable dreams. Now I was sane, I knew what I must do.

I returned to Dave.

I was lost. When I left St Ann's, an arrangement was made for me to attend a local day hospital in Westbourne. I did turn up there, but the place completely freaked me out. It was like St Ann's all over again, peopled with a mixture of wandering, zombie-like patients, stationary, numbed patients and scrupulously distant nurses. Nothing constructive appeared to be happening there. I could see that this was not the way forward. When I failed to return the next day, the staff didn't attempt to find out why.

Luckily, I had a job ready to start, one that I had applied for back in March. I had undergone a gruelling interview procedure to get the job at Marks and Spencer's. Interviews were usually my least favourite thing but I had sailed through this one. This was because in March I had been at the beginning of my slow slide into insanity, at the stage when I was full of phoney self-confidence, bluster and bravado. If I had not been in the throes of mental illness, I would never have got the job. I had impressed my interviewers with a false persona. And since nobody now asked if I had become ill in the interim, I didn't mention my breakdown.

My new employers were presented with a shy, stammering and blushing teenager who bore very little resemblance to the outgoing university student they thought they had employed for her summer break.

I took another job at a local hotel and worked the two together. I was working myself into oblivion, deliberately making myself too tired to think. Work helped me to survive, because it meant I didn't have the time or energy to dwell on my thoughts, and because it made me feel useful. I was needed, if only temporarily, by a hotel owner and some holiday makers. I didn't mind the servility, the humility of my position. It fitted in with my perception of myself.

I went on with my days, like a blinkered workhorse. I was a little more numb than before because of the medication I was taking, but I was cutting down on these drugs already, under the auspices of the psychiatrist. I saw Dr Patel once a month, in the outpatient department at Kings Park Hospital in Boscombe. Another grim location, the waiting room of this clinic, peopled by desperate mutterers and sad murmurers.

I said very little when I went in for these meetings. Just exchanged pleasantries with Dr Patel and told him I wanted to continue to cut down the medication, that I felt much better without it. He had no evidence to the contrary because I wouldn't admit that my nerves were still raw, that I was still terribly anxious. Under his supervision I decreased my medication, and mercifully I didn't relapse into incoherence.

I was still the same person after all, and I decided to continue with the course of action that had been so rudely interrupted by my breakdown. I got in touch with the Dean of the Law Faculty, who agreed that I could return to university to restart my course from the first year. In October of 1988 I returned to the University of Southampton, ready to make the same mistakes all over again.

37
Psychotherapy

I quickly found that it was unwise to talk about my breakdown. On my first day back in the Law Faculty a boy bounded towards me in the Common Room. 'Louise! How are you? Where have you been?' I was nonplussed. I didn't have a clue who he was.

'Simon!' he explained. It meant nothing to me.

'I'm sorry,' I said. 'I have had a nervous breakdown. I was in hospital'. The look in Simon's eyes told me all I needed to know. He never spoke to me again, and in turn I never spoke to anyone at university of my breakdown again. I don't know what I would have said in any case. My illness had not been diagnosed, or explained to me. I had no hook to hang it on, no way of making sense of what had happened, so the easiest course of action was to discard my breakdown and all memories of it. By Christmas I had stopped taking all medication, with the approval of Dr Patel.

I had decided to live in a hall of residence while I re-took my first year of studies. Dave and I spoke on the phone every evening, and I returned home to him every weekend. I phoned my mother too, and my sisters, but she was always drunk, and they were always busy. I sensed that my needy, over-frequent phone calls were an unwanted interruption in their lives.

I coasted through the academic work, since I was only repeating what I had learned during the previous year. Other aspects of the course were much more difficult. I managed to attend lectures, but I found tutorials excruciating. I had a phobia of enclosed spaces, and whatever the size of the classroom, however I tried to position myself, I would start to blush about something or other, which triggered a panic attack, starting as a tight knot in my head, pins and needles spreading outwards. I often reached the point where I thought I might physically explode, and wouldn't have cared if I did.

Thank goodness, this time I asked for help. I was referred by my GP to a psychotherapist, who gave me weekly appointments. He decided that the best method to deal with my phobia of blushing was to avoid the situations that triggered it, so he wrote a letter to the Dean of the Law Faculty excusing me from attendance at any seminars and tutorials.

I led an unusually quiet life for a university student, and the academic year slowly passed. But although the worst of my symptoms stayed away, my nerves were still raw. Panic was only ever a step away and consequently I lived like a cat on a hot brick. Eating lunch in the student refectory with my classmates, I was on tenterhooks in case anyone said anything that triggered a blush. I failed to pay proper attention to the conversation, couldn't join in properly. I never relaxed. I survived at university only because I had to, because I could see no course of action other than to go ahead and complete my degree.

The first year exams came and went, and I acquitted myself reasonably well. By now, I had decided to be honest with myself. I was restless, bored and unhappy. Dave was so perfect, so calm and self-assured. He was not for me. I knew I had to end the relationship, but I was terrified that the insecurity of finding myself alone again would send me over the edge into insanity. I did the only possible thing in the circumstances. I ran away.

38
Israel

It was a calculated flight and I chose an opportune moment. I had passed my end of year exams and been signed off by the psychologist.

Leaving Dave meant leaving his house, and I had nowhere to go. I didn't want to ask my family for help or a place to stay, although a lot of them still lived in Bournemouth. Belita and Jane both had growing families and busy lives, and Stephen still lived with my mother. I knew I could never stay with them again.

Mandy was still abroad, but she came to my aid, lending me £500 for the air fare to Israel, where she had arranged for one of her friends from Kibbutz Revivim to meet me at the airport. She had also arranged for me to stay at Revivim for the summer, until I could return to university for the next academic year.

At that time, Revivim had up to a hundred 'volunteers', or temporary workers, each summer. A kibbutz is basically a commune, and Revivim was large, with about six hundred permanent residents. In the summer, extra help was needed, mainly to harvest the fruit crops, but also to work in the kitchens or laundry, the plastics factory, or with the chickens or cows and so on.

Young people volunteered to work for a pittance, with free room and board, knowing they would have time to sunbathe, swim and socialise. It was a great way to spend a summer.

I shared a room with two other English girls, Laura and Madeleine, who had come to the kibbutz together. They were very welcoming. I was not put off by the accommodation. Although three of us shared one room, it was clean, and in many ways better than some of the bedsits I'd inhabited during my dismal, late teenaged years. At least there was no question of having to find coins to feed the meter.

The kibbutz was green and lush. If you arrived there from outer space, you would never guess that it was located in the middle of the Negev desert. Revivim was an oasis. The volunteer accommodation was simple but the families lived in pleasant, modern homes and all the residents benefitted from a library, cinema and theatre, a clubhouse, swimming pool and other amenities. As far as I was concerned, it was luxury. Nirvana.

On the kibbutz, my social fears lessened. I was shy, I still blushed, but there were less occasions to trigger my fears. I loved to sit outside around the campfire with the other volunteers, listening to the songs and conversations. Life seemed a lot more carefree at this distance from home.

I was taken under the wing of a lovely family. Dalia and Ramy were Mandy's 'adoptive parents', allocated to set her at ease when she had first arrived on the kibbutz. Now they looked after me. I knew that I was welcome to visit their home. Most Friday evenings I walked over to their rooms to eat Dalia's wonderful cake before we all went to the dining room together. The apartment was always packed with family and friends talking, joking and eating.

I worked hard. I had been allocated to go to the 'Lul', the chicken houses. I got up at four thirty each morning to start work at the Lul at five. It was a mile or two away from the kibbutz and the eight or ten of us who worked there headed out on a tractor. It was cold in the desert at

175

this time of day, bumping along the rough tracks. When we arrived we showered and then changed into our working clothes, to avoid cross contamination to or from the birds.

There were ten large chicken sheds, each crammed with literally thousands of birds. These chickens, in vast numbers, were really noisy. To collect their eggs, I had to clear a path as I walked, moving chickens out of the way with my feet. I was desperate not to harm them, although their lives seemed to be hardly worth living anyway. It was stressful work and also incredibly hot, too hot to breathe. Whatever air I managed to suck in was filled with dust and feathers.

I spent three hours each morning gathering eggs. When a hen was still roosting, I used one hand to gently lift her, then slid the other underneath to steal her egg. She was toasty, unnervingly warm. She almost felt as if she mattered. We then showered, changed our clothes and returned to the kibbutz for breakfast. After breakfast, we went back for another shower and a further three hours of hard slog.

It wasn't easy, especially starting so early in the morning and working for so long before breakfast, but after another shower and lunch it was still only midday, and then my time was my own. I snoozed by the swimming pool most afternoons, trying to get a suntan, or showed off by speeding up and down it. I was still unutterably vain. I would not countenance removing my contact lenses when I swam, and thus I lived in fear of losing them.

I got a lot of male attention in the early days at Revivim. Israeli men are the handsomest in the world, and there was never a shortage of young Israelis approaching me in the dining room to introduce themselves, with the opening line that my sister had been their good friend. As a result, Mandy went up higher than ever in my estimation.

I was determined not to embark on any romances. After all, I had only just disentangled myself from Dave. Clearly, the correct course of action was to remain single for the summer, since I would be returning to university at the end of that time.

This sensible attitude lasted for at least a week. One evening by the blazing campfire, I found myself in the grip of a Belgian lad. A kiss can be enough, and one rather wet kiss from this boy informed me that he was definitely not for me. As I managed to wriggle out of his incredibly persistent embrace, I looked up to meet the piercing eyes of a man approaching our circle laden down with baggage.

It was another Belgian, Alexander. He turned out to be a veteran volunteer who had been to Revivim on many previous occasions. He was also the university lecturer of Georges, the boy whose kiss I had been suffering. Alexander was twenty-eight, incredibly tall and muscular, and I was instantly smitten. I could not have encountered this person at a worse moment in my life. I knew from that awful start that he was out of my reach, but I never stopped yearning for him.

I dismissed Georges, who promptly spread a rumour that I had jumped on him and forcibly snogged him by the campfire. I didn't care. I flirted with Alexander all summer. I wanted him so badly and there were moments when I thought I was in with a chance. But, although we once or twice played surreptitious footsie under the dining room table and I managed one glorious slow dance with him at a party, nothing else ever happened. I reluctantly concluded that he was not interested in me, but for the remainder of the summer I never switched my attentions to anybody else. There would have been no point.

In any case, the summer was over all too soon. The volunteers were drifting away. Alexander was returning to his university, to teach the autumn semester. I was due to leave too, but I was reluctant to go. I was dreading the cold rain and dark evenings of Southampton, and the inevitable advent of all my old problems.

I flew back to England, but only to arrange with my tutors to take a year out from my course. They agreed readily with my proposal to continue with my studies the following year. During this short trip home, I stayed with Jane and Tony, doing my best to impress my sister and brother-in-law with descriptions of my adventures abroad and of the friends I had made. I doubt I convinced them. They knew me too well.

I returned to the kibbutz and, with Alexander gone for good, I soon found myself a boyfriend. Yoel was in the army, young, strong and good looking. He was gorgeous in fact, and also sweet and loving. I had fallen on my feet this time.

39
Yoel, and the Ulpan

I grew to love Yoel. The two of us were the picture of young love in fact, a definite and acknowledged item on the kibbutz. He was part of an army group known as the 'Gurin', which comprised around fifty girls and boys who were spending the first six months of their army service on the kibbutz. They would spend the last six months at the kibbutz too, and because of this 'easy year' they served an extra total of six months in the army. The boys served three and a half years in total, the girls two and a half.

The benefit to the kibbutz, apart from the cheap labour, was the chance that some members of the group would decide to make the kibbutz their permanent home. That way, the membership of the kibbutz would be assured into the next generation. This was necessary because a large proportion of the young people who grew up on kibbutzim, not only Revivim but all of them, left after finishing school or university to live or work in the towns, or travel elsewhere, and never returned.

In October of 1989 I was accepted onto the 'Ulpan' course at Revivim. I was now an official student of the Hebrew language. The Ulpan was a facility provided by the kibbutz for people who intended to settle in Israel. I had never declared this intention, but it was assumed. As an Ulpan student, you only had to work half the usual hours in return for your keep, three days a week instead of the usual six. The remaining days were allocated for study. It sounded like a good prospect to me.

At that time there were two Hebrew classes in Revivim, Beginners and Advanced. I was admitted to the upper class, by virtue of the fact that I had already spent a summer on the kibbutz and had learned a smattering of the language.

The students arrived en masse. There were forty of us in total. Most of the students were new immigrants to Israel, and the others were generally applying for residency. They were a colourful bunch of people.

Most of the seasonal work on the kibbutz had finished by the time the volunteers had gone, because the bulk of it had been in the fields, and by now the crops had been harvested. Our work, therefore, was mostly in the factory, the laundry and the kitchens.

I had a few strokes of luck. Firstly, I was chosen to work with the children, which was the best job I could have hoped for. I loved children, and for me the opportunity to work with them was not really work at all. After the noise and smell of the chicken sheds, the company of these children was bliss. I had the added benefit of being able to learn Hebrew as I worked. I was learning at the level of a two-year-old, but this helped me to pick up the basics quickly. I needed to communicate with the children, and it gave me the confidence to speak Hebrew out loud.

I picked up the new language from my co-workers and the children. I read 'The Hungry Caterpillar' for them in English or Hebrew and they filled in the gaps.

'And so he ate four...'

'Arbaah...'

'Strawberries!'

'Agvaniot!'

My kibbutz 'mother', Dalia, helped immensely. She would (perhaps could) only speak to me in Hebrew, so I learned new words from her whenever I saw her.

Next, after my change from working with chickens to working with children, I was asked to take on the position of work manager to the volunteers. This was in addition to my job with the children, and was not arduous. I was a go-between, passing messages and instructions from the kibbutz work manager to the Ulpanists and the few volunteers who remained after the summer. I had a meeting with Nitzan, the work manager, for a few minutes each morning to discuss who was to work where and draw up a timetable so that the students could see what they were doing and when. In reality there was no need for any discussion. Nitzan simply told me who was doing what, and I wrote it down.

I was also supposed to tell the work manager if anybody had a problem with his or her job. In this way, I met someone who would become one of my best friends. She was also called Louise, another Ulpanist. She was the same age as me, and had arrived in Israel as a new immigrant with her husband. Louise was working in the kitchen, hated her job and was being bullied by one of her co-workers. She complained to me, and when I relayed her problems to Nitzan, he immediately moved her to a position she relished, working with children of a slightly younger age group than mine. Louise was so grateful for this change of work that I made myself a friend for life.

There were two French girls who were not so lucky. They were delicate, fastidious types who had been sent to work in the Lul and hated every moment of it. Their disgust of the chickens was so extreme that it was funny. They both appealed to me daily, but the work manager was totally unmoved and refused to change their jobs.

After a few weeks I stopped trying to ask him, but the two girls never stopped begging me to intervene. It got to the point where I was frightened to face them each day, knowing that I was powerless to help.

I found, to my dismay, that when all the students had arrived and the classes started, my old difficulties returned. The classroom situation set off my paranoia, and the blushing phobia came flooding back. Looking back, I don't know why this surprised me. I had never addressed the cause of my problems, so there was no reason why they should have vanished. I had been alright on the kibbutz during the summer, when we were mostly working outdoors, but being in close proximity to other people in the Hebrew lessons turned out to be a trigger for my social anxiety.

The first Hebrew class that I attended, the introductory one, was especially embarrassing, and for once I had good reason to blush. We were paired up for an ice-breaker in which we were asked to introduce our partner to the group and tell everybody what we had learned about that person.

My partner was a gawky young English lad called Dean, who had a young Israeli girlfriend. Dean explained to me that although his girlfriend was still at school, he was learning Hebrew with the intention of applying for Israeli citizenship so that he could stay with her. As part of the process, he had to convert to Judaism. Then Dean began to confide in me about the circumcision that he would have to undergo to become a Jew. He went into great anatomical detail about all the pros and cons of possessing a foreskin and the potential pain of the operation. I tried to listen politely, but all I could think about was how red in the face I had become, and how dreadful this made me feel. The experience seemed to last forever.

Eventually our teacher, Alon, a wonderful, gentle man, told us that it was time to continue with the next part of the exercise and recount to the group all that we had found out about our new friends. I was paralysed with fear. If I had been offered the world in return, I could not have spoken out loud about Dean's dilemma regarding the process of dispensing with his foreskin. The problem was that I couldn't think up any other information to share about him.

By the time my turn arrived, I was shaking with nerves. What I wanted to say was, 'Dean talked for so long about his penis that I hardly found out anything about him'. Instead, I blurted out, 'Dean is English and he wants to make his home in Israel.' Then I sat miserably looking downwards at the desk in front of me, sweating and crimson.

This session set the scene for future Hebrew classes. I was friendly enough with my fellow students outside lesson time, but so self-conscious in the classes that I could hardly concentrate on what we were taught. I was too occupied with listening for someone to say something that might set off the blushing and make me a spectacle, and of course this meant that I was a permanent bundle of nerves with a blush waiting to happen.

On the Ulpan course were some American students, some French, and a smattering from other countries. There were a lot of Russians. They all studied diligently. A lot of them were new immigrants with no resources at all, and they needed to learn the language as quickly as possible so they could start earning a living.

The weather gradually changed. The days were warm but no longer stifling, and the desert nights became surprisingly cold. I loved learning about the history of Israel and we were often taken on trips to see special places around the country. I have always found religion and politics to be difficult subjects, because both sides of an argument often appear to me to be equally valid, but during my time on the Ulpan I grew to understand fully why the Jewish people needed a land of their own and why they were willing to fight to hold on to it.

My daily routine altered as the long, hot summer finally ended. Life was still interesting, at times exciting, but there was not so much of a party atmosphere. I also began to feel a little frustrated about the language. Hebrew is a straightforward language, phonetically spoken and spelled, with a vocabulary of only about 6,000 words, which is tiny compared to the 60,000 or so to be found in the Oxford English dictionary.

I was learning fairly rapidly, considering that I spent no time studying. I could follow basic conversations, and occasionally take part in them. However, I could not understand the more advanced Hebrew spoken on television or the radio. I could not read a national or local newspaper, or understand what was happening in the kibbutz by perusing the general notice board. I missed the complexities of the English language and hated lacking the ability to devour written words wherever I was. In truth, I was homesick for my mother tongue.

The kibbutz had an English library, which was surprisingly well stocked. This meant that I could at least indulge my reading habit. It was the kibbutz library that introduced me to John Steinbeck, Paul Gallico and Alan Sillitoe, who remain some of my favourite authors. But meanwhile I was getting edgy in the Hebrew classes. I felt that I was on display and being mocked. On one level I knew it was ridiculous to assume that anybody paid any attention to me but then again, I knew that the blushing did make me conspicuous. Real life had crept into the holiday mood.

Despite all this I had no concerns about my mental health. There was a doctor on the kibbutz, but it never occurred to me to ask him for help. To me, nerves were normal, and any period of time that I was free from them was an anomaly.

It helped that I developed a strong friendship with my room-mate. Clare was English and we found a lot to talk about. We came from different backgrounds. She was privileged, in my eyes, to come from a close nuclear family. But we still had a lot in common. We were both searching, in some way, both at a junction in our lives. We had both gone to Israel, I think, to find ourselves.

I made Clare laugh with stories about my childhood. I told her of the time when my friend Debbie, visiting although my father had banned her from our house, had to hide quaking under my bed when he returned unexpectedly from the casino. From her hiding place she'd heard him swear me to secrecy as he confided his 'deepest secret ever', which luckily for us all turned out to be some nonsense about my supposedly promiscuous sister Mandy. I told her about Dad's awful driving, and about how he peed in a chamber pot at night and made my mother empty the orange, stinking mess each morning.

And his chain-smoking. I recounted the tale to Clare of how my father would sit in his armchair, lost in thought, with a long, longer, impossibly long cylinder of dead cigarette creeping down to the filter held between his fingertips. And how we yelled at him, 'Ash, Dad, ash!', only to watch in despair as he slowly turned to look at us, making the incredible structure fall and dissolve into the rest of the muck that lived on our carpets. It was strange to talk about my family after so many years of silence and it felt disloyal, even at a distance, but it was a huge relief to be able to laugh about it all.

I started to write funny poems from time to time, especially as little 'goodbyes' when friends left the kibbutz. I did a fair amount of drawing too, copies of pictures I had seen, to illustrate these poems. These drawings somehow came to the attention of those in charge of the kibbutz, with the result that for a couple of weeks I was given the task of working full time, copying and colouring Disney pictures to decorate one of the children's houses.

One evening Clare and I were discussing the traits and peculiarities of some of our fellow students, and I wrote a series of short poems sending them up. We crept to the Ulpan common room in the night and pinned them up on the notice board. The next morning brought differing reactions from the students. Some found the poems amusing, some were upset. I was delighted, although puzzled, to find my teacher Alon not only chuckling over the verses, but taking photographs of them. I wondered what he intended to do with these, and I never found out.

Clare left the kibbutz shortly after the Ulpan ended, and so did most of the other Ulpanists. I clung on in Revivim for a few months longer. Louise was still there. Unfortunately her marriage had ended, but she was determined to remain in Israel anyway. She told me that her father lived in Bournemouth, and asked me to visit him when I returned home.

Yoel and his army group had left the kibbutz too by now, but he visited whenever he could. Our love affair was bitter-sweet. One weekend we were together at his family's flat in Ashdod and I was overcome with sadness because he had to return to duty the next day. I told Yoel how I felt and he held me in his arms as I wept. He said he would not return, but I insisted that he must. I knew that if he did not return to duty when he was expected, he would be sent to prison as a deserter.

The next morning I waved him off from Ashdod to his army bus. He was upset, but I was resolute. He must disregard me and do his duty. I took a different bus. I had decided to spend the day in a museum in Jerusalem, before returning to the kibbutz. I was aghast when I turned a corner in the museum to see Yoel, still in uniform. He had left his group before they reached the army bus, and returned to me.

I was not acting the night I wept and clung to him. My tears had been real enough. But I had never intended for him to turn back. He spent time in military prison for that, and it was my fault. I was embedded deep in this relationship, and it reached its climax the night before I left Israel.

I was due to return to my studies at university. I would be starting the second year of my law degree course. Yoel and I were in the 'Moadon', the kibbutz clubroom. He was trying to speak but the words wouldn't make it out of his mouth, and when he did manage to emit a sound, it was a high-pitched squeak. He sounded as if he had been inhaling helium. When I finally absorbed his words, I was astonished. 'Will you marry me?' my handsome Israeli soldier squeaked. I laughed out loud. Then suddenly I realised that the room had gone quiet. Everyone in the packed club was listening.

My boyfriend had proposed. Our romance was coming to a public conclusion. But sadly, I knew that the only possible answer was no. I knew I was not ready for marriage. Not to Yoel, or to anyone. In fact, I had known for some time that this relationship was not going to last much longer. Yoel, however, clearly did not know this. How could I let down my soldier and burst our beautiful bubble? I wavered. I hesitated.

And then finally I said, because everyone in the room was waiting to hear it, 'Yes. But not now. In the future. Sometime. Thank you. Sorry.' I babbled. I prevaricated. I deliberately misled. And then the next day I returned to my English university. From confusion, in confusion, to yet deeper confusion.

40
Hillel

When I arrived back in England, I went straight to Southampton. It was the start of the university term, but I had nowhere to live. I headed to the student union to try to find housing and as I stood looking at the notice board, I was besieged by loneliness. I felt sorry for myself, and sure that I was the only person in the world with this particular set of problems. I was a student who had come from no home and had no home to return to. I had made friends in my year group twice, and twice left them behind. The friends I had made in my first year had all graduated now and those I knew from my 'second' first year had moved up and on. I had to start over.

I was not entitled to a place in a hall of residence because I was a second-year student. Second years generally lived together in shared houses or in flats. But I had no connections in my year group, and all their living arrangements had been made at the end of the previous year while I was in Israel. The student union accommodation office told me I had missed the boat and it was too late for them to help me find anywhere to live.

There were a few adverts for accommodation on the notice board but none of them seemed viable. I was unsure when my grant would be sorted out, and private rents were payable throughout the year, unlike the halls of residence where you only paid rent during term time. Average private rents were also up to £50 a week, on top of which you had to find money for food and bills. My grant, when it arrived, would only be for £600 a term.

I felt the old, familiar panic beginning to spread through me. I was close to tears. Then I saw a short, simple notice. 'Room available in shared house, £25 a week, kosher kitchen.' There must be a catch, I thought. But I rushed to the nearest phone and dialled the number. A girl answered immediately. She had a posh, plummy tone of voice. 'Yes, we have a room free. In fact, you can have your pick of six. But…' she sounded hesitant, 'You do realise that you have to be Jewish to live here?'

I was taken aback. I hadn't registered the 'kosher' requirement as anything but a stipulation that students should keep the kitchen clean and tidy. But for once I managed to give the appropriate response. 'I didn't' I said. 'But I am.' I wasn't sure the girl believed me but I arranged to go straight to the house, Hillel House, which wasn't far from the university.

I convinced Sam and Lisa, the girls who lived in Hillel House, that I was genuine. I confessed that although I had Jewish blood I had no idea of the rules of kosher living, and they reassured me that the only concession they made themselves was to keep to a vegetarian diet in the house. Hillel House was owned by a trust set up for the benefit of Jewish university students, which was why the rent was so cheap. This year it was very under-subscribed. I really did have my pick of six rooms.

The accommodation was luxurious by student standards. My new home was three storeys tall, with a bathroom on each floor. We had a washing machine. We had a fridge each. Crockery and cutlery was all provided. The house was centrally heated, toasty warm, and there was plenty of hot water.

To top it all, we had a cleaner. Ted came in every morning to do our washing-up, hoovering and other housework. This way, our patrons reasoned, we would have more time to spend on our studies.

The room I chose, at the top of the house, was spacious, with an original wooden floor which was mostly covered by a beautiful, patterned rug. Sam, for some reason, had selected the smallest room in the house, also on the second floor, and Lisa lived alone on the first floor, in a room as big as most other students' whole houses.

Lisa and Sam were graduate students, both taking a master's course in Jewish Studies but I soon realised that they were far more interested in the ways of the world than in their studies. In many ways they were the worst possible housemates for me, since they seemed to be obsessed with sex, and indulged in some of the most lurid conversations I had ever heard. I liked them both a lot, but I was embarrassed in their company and my old blushing phobia surfaced with a vengeance.

Sam had attended private school and been impeccably brought up. She spoke English like an angel. Lisa was more down-to-earth, proud of her working-class roots, with ambitions to become a journalist. She had a long-term boyfriend, David, and claimed that he was the first person she had met who was interested in taking her virginity, although she had been trying to get rid of it since the age of sixteen. I found this hard to believe and it didn't occur to me then that she must have been mixing with a different sort of man than the men I had been associated with.

Lisa claimed to have dyed her pubes a vivid orange, to match the hair on her head, and I thought this must be a lie too because why on earth would anyone want to do that? But one day I was astonished to find the evidence of her veracity, a two-toned pubic hair stuck to the edge of a bathtub.

I kept in touch with Yoel, writing and phoning. We continued to declare our undying love for one another. In Southampton, I hung out with Sam and her friends Robin and Ross, MBA students. We spent days together in cafés and shopping centres and I finally enjoyed the sort of deep conversations I used to think everyone had at university; before, that is, I became a student and realised that most people thought of, and talked about, no more than soap operas and booze.

I felt self-conscious in the company of Ross and Robin. They were both gorgeous to look at. Ross was Greek and Robin was English but with Pakistani parents. They were also both worldly wise, whereas I was well in Sam's shadow socially, still blushing for England. But they didn't seem to mind me tagging along.

Even with the cheap rent at Hillel House, I couldn't make ends meet on my student grant, so I found myself a job, helping in the student canteen. This immediately marked me out as different because none of the other students at Southampton University seemed to need to work. I felt excruciatingly visible in the student canteen, wearing a long checked overall, serving other students their food or working on the till. I worked in the staff canteen too, and found myself in the peculiar position of serving tea or coffee to tutors who were on their breaks from lectures or seminars that I should have been attending.

I enjoyed studying law, although some of the more macabre cases in criminal law played on my mind. I had an over-active imagination. The biggest problem with studying law was that I knew it was wasted on me because I could never in a million years be a lawyer. I was too nervous and shy to string a sentence together. I put this fact to the back of my mind, nurturing a vague hope that at some point during my degree course I would undergo a personality change and become confident and articulate.

The security of Hillel, of having a home, helped to get me through the days. I spent a lot of time in the Law Library. I liked it there. I arrived early and sat at a luxuriously oversized desk by a big window, the Independent newspaper spread out before me, and spent an enjoyable hour reading it. Then I did some perfunctory work, usually mindless copying of headnotes (summaries) of the cases we had been instructed to read.

If I decided I could face a tutorial (I skipped most of them) I did some proper work because I needed to be properly prepared in case I was asked a question. I couldn't countenance the thought of everyone staring at me while I fumbled for an answer, getting ever redder in the face. I also worked properly on my essays. We were given three or four of these a term, and they were assessed. I enjoyed writing them, especially the occasions when had a 'eureka' moment, drawing my own conclusions from a complicated set of facts, knowing that I had come up with something original.

To my surprise, my old crony Clare from Israel arrived on the scene. We'd stayed in touch since she left the kibbutz. She had returned to England when the Ulpan finished, and then spent some time living with her parents in Hampshire while completing a secretarial course. She then found herself a position as a PA in Southampton and a room in a shared house in the road next to mine.

When I introduced Robin and Ross to Clare they were immediately smitten. Clare seemed to have this effect on every man who met her. Soon, however, she met Paul, a New Zealander who lived in the same house as her, and it was clear to everybody that this pair were meant for each other. Before long they left Southampton to travel the world together. I was a friend down.

Hillel House was the meeting place for the Jewish student club, and each week they descended upon us for their Friday night meal. Lisa, Sam and I did not intrude on these meetings. They were no trouble, bringing all the food along with them, cooking and clearing up for themselves. There weren't many members. One of the keenest and most regular was a chap called Dan Diamant, who was in the final year of his course, Aeronautical and Astronautical Engineering.

Sam liked Dan. She confided in me on many occasions that she had a crush on him. What did I think of Dan, she asked. 'He's a dork', I proclaimed disdainfully, and she didn't mention him again.

My second year of studies was drawing to a close. I connected briefly with some other students on my course when I volunteered to take part in an inter-university mooting competition, in which participants simulate court hearings. The first round was scheduled to take part in Scotland, which was the only reason I had any interest in the proceedings. I had a friend from Bournemouth called Dean, who was at Stirling University. I decided that a university-funded jaunt would be an excellent excuse to spend some time with him in Scotland, so I offered to be research assistant to the moot team. I undertook the necessary research and travelled to Scotland as a reserve member of the Southampton Law Team.

The other members of the team were not impressed by my lack of commitment to the competition, especially when I told them my real reason for wanting to be in Scotland. I had a nice holiday in Glasgow, where our team lost the moot, then I visited Dean for a few days afterwards.

The end of the academic year was approaching. I had been a lazy student and had a lot of work to do to catch up with the others. I managed to do it by devoting the whole of the summer term, right up to the exams, to pure revision. I did a huge amount of reading and note-taking, and pulled all the strings together. I achieved respectable but not outstanding exam results. I was on track, I thought, for a lower second-class degree.

This bothered me. Whether I was going to be able to use it or not, my vanity dictated that I wanted a good class of degree. However, unless I did really well in my final year, it looked unlikely that I was going to get one.

In any case, the second year of my course was finally over. I said goodbye to Sam and Lisa. They had both finished their master's courses and received their degrees and they left Southampton to commence their post-student lives. I arranged with the board of trustees that I could return to Hillel at the start of the following term, so the scene was set for me to return to university in the autumn of 1991, for the final year of my studies.

41
The Warden

During the short university holidays I had stayed at Hillel House, funded by my work for the university catering department. I had nowhere to live for the summer, so I visited Yoel in Israel. I spent most of my holiday on the kibbutz without him, though, because he only had a few days of leave from the army. He came straight to the kibbutz for his leave and then we went to visit his family in Ashdod for a day or two, before he returned to duty.

Our reunion was passionate, but internally I felt withdrawn and detached. I was not the same young girl, and he was not the boy I had first met. Both of us had been changed by our separate experiences over the past year. But I still couldn't bear to let him down, so again there was no conclusion to our relationship. It was Dave and Louise all over again.

I was soon back in Southampton. I felt lucky to have Hillel House to return to. I still tried to cling to my family in Bournemouth, to root myself in with them. But my brother and sisters and my mother were too busy with their own lives and attendant problems to take any interest in me and mine. And sadly we had all learned to avoid my father as much as we could. He was rapidly growing older, poorer and thinner and the decline was difficult to witness, but his temper was as brittle as ever.

Really, there was no person who needed me in England. I had no place in the world. I only had to be in Southampton for my university course, which I knew would never result in a legal career anyway. When I was in Israel my home was Kibbutz Revivim and in England it was Hillel House but otherwise I was rootless. I had nothing and nobody, or so I believed.

Hillel House was changing. The trustees had been busy drumming up interest in the accommodation, and consequently the house was filled to capacity from the start of my third year.

In fact, it was chock-a-block with students. There were no longer any spare rooms. There were five first-year male students, and Dan Diamant, who was starting a postgraduate course, also moved in. Then there was me and another girl, Alex, who was also in her final year, studying biology. Her father was chairman of the Hillel House board. I didn't like Alex. She was pretty, confident and in my opinion spoiled and snobbish. We didn't have a lot in common.

Our cleaner and handyman, Ted, had been laid off on the grounds that he was inefficient. I was indignant on his behalf. Ted had taken over the cleaning job from his wife after she died, and although he was getting on in years, he worked to the best of his ability. Lisa, Sam and I had appreciated his presence and his efforts.

But there was no holding back the tides of change. To add insult to injury as far as I was concerned, Alex was nominated as 'Warden' by the board and was allowed to live in the house rent-free. The condition of her appointment was that she ensured that the rest of us kept the place tidy and adhered to the house rules, in particular the keeping of a kosher kitchen.

I was offended by this clear display of nepotism. The situation in Hillel quickly deteriorated under Alex's charge. Sam, Lisa and I may not have been religiously observant, but we had kept to the rules, and only ever had vegetarian food in Hillel. We had also kept the house reasonably clean, with Ted's assistance. Now, within a month of the start of the university term, Hillel became filthy. No-one ever washed up. There was also no effort to keep kosher, and Alex was the worst offender. She cooked roast meals for her boyfriend two or three times each week, and the meat was never kosher.

Alex's behaviour bugged me. I was also jealous of her free tenure. The injustice of it rankled. I was the only resident of Hillel who had already been there for a year. I was working harder than ever in the student refectory to make ends meet. I felt that if anybody should be 'Warden' and live rent-free at Hillel House then they should put in some effort to deserve that title. Really, if anybody should be 'Warden', it should be me, I thought.

The other students muttered about Alex behind her back, but I was more open in my objections. She ignored my complaints, and I lost my cool. I wrote a long letter to the Board of Trustees outlining the situation at Hillel and the reasons why it was unacceptable. Every other tenant, except of course Alex, read it through and signed their names and I sent it off.

But I was innocent in the ways of politics, and ill-prepared for what was to follow. I was summoned to attend a meeting of the board of trustees and meanwhile, the first-year students who had signed the letter panicked. They were all castigated by their parents for potentially compromising their tenancies. They claimed they hadn't meant to sign or hadn't read the letter properly. They distanced themselves from me.

I attended the meeting with the only other student who was strong enough to stand by his word and back me up in the allegations I had made against Alex, Dan Diamant. He was doing a master's in International Politics. Dan was the chap Sam had had a crush on at the end of the previous year when he was finishing his first degree. I was grateful for Dan's support and sure that with his help justice would prevail.

We arrived at Bournemouth, where the board was based, for the meeting. I was taken aback by the formality of it. We sat around a long table, headed by Alex's father, the chairman. The other members of the board were elderly and distinguished and all looked very serious. It felt as if I was the witness at a legal enquiry, rather than a student complaining about difficulties with her accommodation.

Alex turned up with her mother, looking as if butter wouldn't melt in her mouth. Then the board commenced questioning me. They said they were attempting to establish the truth. Alex lied smoothly and fluently. She made counter accusations against me, none of them based remotely upon fact, all to the effect that I was morally degenerate.

Dan stood firm and remained calm, but I went to pieces. I blushed, stammered, struggled unsuccessfully to defend myself. I was the image of guilt. The upshot of this farce was that Alex remained firmly in place as Warden and I came out as the villain of the piece who had spread lies and gossip about an innocent girl. I wasn't the witness at a legal enquiry, I was the accused and I had been found fully culpable. I was astonished, but helpless against the glaring injustice.

The only upside was that this turned out to be the start of a new relationship, with Dan Diamant. Until that point, I had thought of Dan as slightly odd, a little too strait-laced and single-minded to be normal. He was

Israeli, but had been educated in an English public school. His father worked for the United Nations. Dan was totally committed to anything he took on. He was a black belt in karate, head of the university juggling club and a leading light of the university debating society. He seemed too good to be true, so measured that even his sense of humour seemed studied.

Now that we were sharing a home, I'd got to know him better and appreciated his qualities more. We'd become friends, and for some reason we regularly went to the local casino together. We were often out until the early hours.

Our first kiss happened at about four o'clock one morning on our return from one of these excursions. We were wedged together into the tiny sofa by the door of the Hillel kitchen. The embrace took the usual course. Dan kissed me, I kissed him back. He stroked my leg, and I caressed his in return. Then he burst into loud song, 'Anything you can do, I can do better...' I dissolved into giggles.

After a few weeks I called Yoel and told him that I had found someone else. I wanted to be honest and I'd known for some time that we didn't have a future together. But when he refused to accept that the break was final, calling me at all hours of the day and night and begging me to reconsider, I felt sorry for him and failed to hold my ground. I was with someone else now, I told him. But maybe I added, in the future, things might change... In other words, I took the coward's path.

Dan and I had a lot of fun together. One weekend we went to Brighton. Dan was keen to see my old school, Roedean, and had already taken me to see his, Canford School in Dorset. I stood at the bottom of the hill that led to Roedean, looking up at the beloved building, filled with emotion and longing to go up and see inside.

I was too embarrassed to visit my old school, I told Dan. I had failed in life and my teachers there would only be disappointed in me. He was puzzled by this. I was reading for a law degree. How could this be failure? Why would they not be pleased to see me? I couldn't explain it to him, since I had never told him about my breakdown, but I was convinced that what I believed was the truth. I had left Roedean a golden child, and now I was a shadow of my old self. I had been a mental patient and I was shy, blushing and inadequate in every way.

I was seeing the psychotherapist again at this time, and when he asked if I thought I would marry Dan, I immediately said no. Marriage? What was he thinking? I was only twenty-two. I was a world away from settling down. I explained to the psychotherapist that the situation was not right. I didn't mention that I was still thinking of Yoel and of the possibility of an alternative life on the kibbutz. He was still phoning me regularly, pledging true love, begging me not to let go of what we had. I was worried about what might happen to him if I didn't return. I was caving in to his pleas.

So, as my final year at university drew to a close, I ended both of my relationships. Dan was a good friend and could not be faulted as a boyfriend. But I was tired of it all. I finished with Yoel on the phone and by letter, so he would be left in no doubt that it was final this time. I wanted no more demands on me. I just wanted peace and quiet.

42

The University Catering Department

I knew that when I left university I would miss the colleagues I'd worked with in the student refectory. They were mostly motherly middle-aged women, and I'd felt more comfortable with them than my fellow students. I'd worked for the catering department every day of the week from 3pm to 7pm. I'd worked in the holidays too, waitressing at the conferences the university hosted because I needed to find money for rent and bills out of term time too.

I'd also worked at weekends when I could. On a few occasions I'd waited at the student balls that took place in the union building. The students were often badly behaved, rude, bossy and arrogant towards the staff. It was a glimpse into the class divide.

At one ball, a lad at the Rugby Club table became lewd and suggestive. I blushed and stammered and couldn't think of anything smart and crushing to say in response, although I longed to. I hated the fact that he had made the whole table stare and laugh at me.

Later, the tables were turned. The meal was due to finish early, but the ball would continue into the early hours. I had asked my boss if she would mind me changing into my ballgown and joining the other students after I finished work. She had agreed, and I had arranged to meet Robin, Ross and Sam.

When I joined my friends, powdered and dolled up, I made sure I found the offending student and left him in no doubt that I was a student too. His reaction was perfect. He was shocked and embarrassed, and having elicited the information that I was a law student, apologised profusely for his rudeness. He was a medical student as well as a rugby player, and gross drunkenness was a prerequisite of both occupations, or so he claimed.

I nodded graciously and left the rest unsaid. I hope he would think twice before upsetting another waitress.

I had another unpleasant experience while working in the student refectory. I did not practice any religion, but had thought of myself as Jewish for a long time, especially since living at Hillel. One week in the holidays, the university hosted the 'Conference of Christians and Jews'. One of my fellow waitresses had a grudge against Jews and kept voicing racist diatribes.

I listened miserably to these outbursts of prejudice, too embarrassed to speak up, feeling a total coward for not doing so. Eventually, I confided in another waitress, Sue, a kind lady who I felt sure would not turn against me on the basis that I was Jewish.

Sue was horrified. 'I'll put her in her place,' she promised. I begged her not to make the matter personal. She was calm and immediate in her reaction. At the next opportunity, when the bigot began to speak about the behaviour of the Jews at the conference, Sue said, 'The Jews are the same as the Christians, and if you think differently, you're the one with the problem'.

I was grateful, but also humbled. Despite all my years of study, I had still not learned the essentials of communication, including how and when to speak up for myself. I was an incomplete human being and I knew it.

But I had to put negative thoughts behind me and move on. There was work to be done. As usual near exam time, I needed to immerse myself in revision. In fact, I had a lot more to do than revise, I had whole areas of the law to learn from scratch. I had been detached from the reality of my law studies for most of the previous year. I hardly knew any of my fellow students and hadn't attended a single lecture for most of my courses. This time my revision was tinged with panic. I had no idea whether I could learn all that was expected of me. There was a lot of information to cram into a short space of time. I gave up my work in the catering department and settled down to study.

I was fortunate that in those days at university, at least on my course, there was hardly any assessed work. There were no tests, no other ways of checking if you were keeping up during the year, and this system worked in my favour. My academic strength was my good memory and luckily the last-minute cramming paid off again. I passed all my exams. I got firsts for two modules and upper seconds for another three, although I got a lower second for my dissertation, a half-hearted piece of research into the abuse of children in various institutions. The upshot was that I had enough total credits to qualify for an Upper Second-Class degree. I was redeemed, academically at least.

I was relieved but I still had a sense of failure. I told myself that my teachers at Roedean would have been less than impressed with anything other than a First. I pictured Bobby Robinson tutting over me. When I was eleven, I was earmarked for a First at Oxford, and here I was with a mere Upper Second from Southampton. Added to this, I was 23 already, and my fellow graduates were (mostly) only 21.

Whatever I achieved, it never felt like enough.

I packed my bags to return to Bournemouth. I'd left Hillel House a term earlier, around the time that I split from Dan. I hadn't felt comfortable there after the showdown with Alex, so my last term was spent in a hall of residence. I had no attachments left to any person or place in Southampton, so there were no emotional goodbyes. It was five years since I'd started my three-year law degree and the process was finally over. I left quietly. I had proven my intellect. Now it was only my ability to cope with life that hung in the balance.

43
Stanley's Casino

I was not sorry to leave university behind, but it meant that my life was now hurtling forwards without a plan or a goal. The magical transformation I had hoped for had not taken place and I was no more articulate or confident than I had ever been. I was now nearly 24. I had a law degree but was otherwise no better equipped to be a lawyer than when I first arrived in Southampton as a shy 18-year-old. There was another problem. I had nowhere to live in Bournemouth and no source of income. I had no idea how I would manage.

Then I had a stroke of luck. My sister Jane had been working as a floor waitress in Stanley's, a Bournemouth casino, and they were looking for someone to join the team. Jane put my name forward and I got the post without difficulty. So, armed with a degree in law, and two years' experience in the university catering department, I went to work as a full-time waitress.

It was July 1992 when I started at Stanley's Casino. I worked mostly night shifts from 9pm until 4am, and the occasional day shift from 2pm until 9pm. These jobs were highly sought after because although they were poorly paid, we earned a small fortune in tips. I considered myself lucky to get a place on the team, and to be accepted so easily by the girls I worked with.

I soon picked up the basics. Gamblers needed to eat, but they often became too involved with the gambling to realise this, which was where the floor waitresses came in. We had a small kitchen where we made sandwiches, teas and coffees and soft drinks, which were provided free of charge to the gamblers, or punters as we called them. We placed the refreshments on small side tables which we drew up beside the punters with the minimum of fuss so they could eat and drink without taking their eyes off the game.

A good floor waitress kept her eyes and ears open and quickly learned who the serious and regular gamblers were, who played for big money, and who tipped the best. The refreshments were complimentary but it was customary to tip the waitress who delivered them. It was also smart to tip well, because naturally the bigger tippers got the best and fastest service.

The really big tippers got what they needed before they knew they needed it. Coffee at their sides every half hour, with exactly the right amount of milk and sugar. The best sandwiches with the freshest ingredients. The management even provided free cigarettes for those punters who really liked to gamble big time. And those punters always rewarded the waitress who delivered them.

Interestingly, those gamblers, the ones who were addicted, were the politest and most considerate. They had to be, perhaps, since they spent so much time in the casino and the waitresses were the people who made sure they were comfortable while they were there. The problematic punters, the ones I wanted to curse at 2am on a Sunday morning when my feet and legs were aching to the point of collapse and all I wanted was to fall into my bed, were the young lads, the drunkards, the braggarts. The ones who didn't tip much, if at all. And the girls who hung out with them, who also never tipped. I hated them all.

I quickly grew mercenary. The punters ceased to be people. I viewed them only in terms of how much money they might give me. I saved my best smiles and kindest attention for those who regularly tipped five pounds or more. I was not happy with the person I had become, but it was normal in the casino setting.

Because Jane and I worked in Stanley's, my father was not allowed in, but I knew he was still a regular at the other Bournemouth casinos. It made me sad to think of him wasting his life in the same way as the punters I saw daily wasting theirs. Everything around me, all I perceived, started to take on shades of black.

I squandered every penny I earned. I had rented a flat in Boscombe Crescent. It was unfurnished, equipped only with ancient gas heaters. Boscombe Crescent was the worst area of Bournemouth, or at least the area that had the worst reputation for drugs, thievery and every imaginable type of calumny.

I started mixing with my old friends, Dave's old friends, and smoking dope again. I didn't know what else to do with my free time. I was so lonely. The more I smoked, the more paranoid and freaked out I became, but I persisted with it. Winter drew in and the flat was freezing, but I was so distracted that I hardly noticed. I rarely saw daylight because I was working most nights, then getting home, sleeping, waking up, getting stoned, going into work again. I became half crazed, then more than half crazed.

I'd find a lunatic, druggie boyfriend, dump him and then get another, crazier one. I saw my mother infrequently and the rest of my family hardly at all (except Jane, when we worked a shift together).

I was a mess, and on some level I knew it. I was becoming distraught. While I was at university I'd kept away from cigarettes and dope and this had enabled me to hold on to my sanity. Undoubtedly, the cannabis was a factor in my sudden deterioration, but I was not bright enough to realise it. What I did know was that the best part of a year had passed since my graduation and I still had no idea of where I was heading. I did not know what to do next. I was lost and unhappy, my relationships kept crashing and I was working in a dead-end job that was making me miserable. There was no reason to be in Bournemouth and yet there I was.

So I made a decision. I would become a solicitor after all. I would borrow £5000 to pay for a postgraduate course at the College of Law, and get myself a career and a decent life.

44

The College of Law

I was losing the plot. My latest 'decision' was no more than a delusion. I was as nervous and shy as I had ever been. I had trouble coping as a waitress, so I don't know how I decided I could manage as a student again, considering that my most anguished moments over the years had been in the classroom.

I hadn't thought my plan through at all. I'd chosen to attend the College of Law at Chester, since I liked the sound of the city, but I had no money for accommodation or living expenses. I didn't have a penny, in fact, beyond the £5000 I'd borrowed on a student loan for the course fees. However, the fees were payable in two instalments, in September and January, which I thought might buy me some time. I was sure I could wing it. The course only lasted nine months ,after all, and I could find waitressing work to keep myself going, as I'd done at university. I convinced myself that all this was perfectly feasible.

I didn't have much of an awareness of mental illness or its symptoms, despite my stay at St Ann's Hospital. Since I'd left there five and a half years previously, I hadn't given my breakdown much thought. In fact, I had deliberately blanked it out of my mind. If I considered it at all, I was sure that those days were behind me.

I had no idea at all that I was unwell. Instead, I fooled myself into thinking that I had at last magically transformed into the confident and articulate person I longed to be, perfectly suited to a career in law.

When I arrived at Chester I was, on the surface, one of the more outgoing and sociable students. I was always out in the evenings, chatting away to someone. In fact I was manic, and fast spiralling out of control.

I made friends at law school rapidly. The other students were polite, and diligent in their studies. I, by contrast, threw myself into all the extra-curricular activities. I attended all the Law Society social events. I joined the chess club. I signed up for a parachute jump in aid of charity, which was due to take place early the following term. I felt capable of anything, and even managed to devote some of my boundless energy to my studies. I did reasonably well in the assessed work, and took careful notes in class.

But I had no real awareness of what was happening. My concentration was slipping. I got a cold, which developed into a cough and a chest infection. I coughed and hacked my way noisily through classes, almost delirious. Antibiotics failed to cure the infection. I was worn to the edge with this illness, and vaguely aware that the other students were getting irritated with me for disturbing the classes, but I managed to ignore this. Meanwhile, at the edges of my consciousness, paranoia was creeping in.

I lodged with a local family near the Law College and managed to pay the rent by getting a part-time job at a local hotel and by borrowing from the bank. Even so, my funds ran out before the first half of the first term. I was nonplussed. Now what? I had not seen my older brother Mike since I was little, but I knew he lived nearby. I decided I would move in with him and his wife and commute daily to college, about an hour's drive on the motorway. Luckily for me, my brother agreed. He didn't want any money for rent or board, and he provided me with petrol for my journeys to college.

I'd always been a nervous driver, and I hated driving on motorways. But now, amazingly, I felt no fear at all. It was another welcome manifestation of my new, confident persona. And it seemed reasonable behaviour to race my car, an ancient Morris Minor, up and down to Chester every day on the motorway, blithely expecting that it would thrive on constant and extended use.

Of course, it didn't. The Moggy was suffering from exhaustion like me, and one day on the M54 it gave up the ghost. My brother came to my rescue again, sent someone to collect me and put another of his friends to work on installing a reconditioned engine in my old car. Meanwhile, he lent me a new vehicle to travel to college in.

Despite all the help from my brother and his wife, I began to sense that I was running to a halt. The second half of my fees were due, and I had no money to pay them. I made it to the end of term, although my nerves were in shreds. I had a week off college to revise before the exams and I tried to swot for them, but my brain was not up to the job. I was irrational, my mind continually running off at a tangent. I had stopped smoking when I began law school, but restarted the habit, and spent most of my evenings standing outside the kitchen door, cigarette glowing in the dark, gazing up at the stars. I ate the abundant meals that my brother's wife cooked daily, plus everything I could forage from the huge pantry. Strangely, I only became skinnier. I could not eat enough to make the fuel that my mind was burning.

I took one humiliating oral exam then I couldn't stand it any longer. I bowed out of law school. I left without explaining anything to my new friends, because

I didn't know how to tell them that I thought I was going mad.

My brother didn't realise that I was unwell any more than I did, and couldn't understand why I was throwing in the towel. I told him there was no way I could continue with the course. I headed back to Bournemouth, with no idea what I would do when I got there. There was one consolation. At least I didn't have to attempt that bloody parachute jump.

45

The Royal Bath

Back in Bournemouth, I had to find somewhere to live and a way to survive financially. When I moved to Chester, I had sublet my flat to a couple that I worked with at Stanley's Casino, both of them croupiers, and so I evicted them and moved back in.

The flat was a dump, but I considered it to be my home. All the furniture, carpets and curtains were second-hand. The rooms were large, with only basic heating. The place was not properly self-contained. I shared a front door with the upstairs flat, and my hallway was open to their stairs, so I could not move between my own rooms in private. But I had a home.

I heard through the grapevine that a floor waitress was needed at another local casino, the Grosvenor, which was based at the Royal Bath Hotel, a five-star establishment on Bournemouth seafront.

I had missed my old mates from Stanley's, and so I thought the ideal solution to my immediate financial troubles would be to go back to the same line of work. I got the job and became friendly with another waitress, Claire. We were the same age, both single, and often went out drinking together.

Claire had worked at the Royal Bath, as everyone called the Grosvenor Casino, for some time. She knew my dad, who had been a regular punter for many years. He was barred now that I worked there, which was a relief. I was an adult, but I was still scared of him.

Claire, on the other hand, said she found my father amusing, and she liked him. I assumed that was because he tipped well but she said he was interesting and quirky. It was a shock to me when it sank in that my father's revolting habits, like the chain smoking, were considered by my friend to be merely harmless and amusing facets of his character.

Claire told me that when my Dad gambled he often had two cigarettes simultaneously smoking in ashtrays beside him; he became so carried away that he forgot he was smoking one and lit another. I found this repugnant, but to her it was 'rather sweet'. I was grateful, for reasons I didn't understand, to be speaking to someone who thought well of my father.

Adam, the cashier at the Royal Bath, also spoke about my dad. He told me a story of a time when Dad had cashed in some chips at the end of the evening, and complained that Adam had short-changed him by £50. He'd made Adam count up the whole night's takings there and then, to be sure. When Adam reached this point in his anecdote I interrupted, cringing with embarrassment, and apologetically said that my dad was obsessed with money and should have taken Adam's word for it.

'No,' the cashier admitted. 'The old bugger was right. I'd made a mistake.' Adam told it with admiration, the fact that my father had calculated correctly and had been bolshy enough to make him double check. Again, I couldn't help but be touched that somebody had praised my dad, although again I was confused that I felt this way.

Claire and I often went out to drink at a little bar opposite the casino, on Westover Road. I turned 25, and we celebrated. I never overdid the drinking. For one thing, I still had my Morris Minor, I drove everywhere in it, and I wouldn't risk losing my licence for the sake of alcohol. Dope was a different matter. It was not illegal to smoke and drive, or if it was, I wasn't aware of it. I was permanently stoned, at work and out of it.

It wasn't many weeks before I ran into trouble at work. I was not myself, maybe due to the dope. I was rude to the customers and thought nothing of answering the managers back if they rebuked me for my behaviour. The night I lost my job, I'd been told to work an extra shift to cover a function. I knew I couldn't refuse outright, but I failed to turn up until two hours into the shift and then made a perfunctory excuse about having trouble with my car. I was as indignant when I was disbelieved as I would have been if I hadn't been lying, and resigned on the spot.

I still had rent to find and bills to pay. I took the first job I could find, as a barmaid at a local pub. It paid very little though, and I had to work flat out to make ends meet. I could hardly keep my act together.

For some reason I left that job and went to work as a barmaid at another pub instead. I was struggling to get up in the mornings, struggling to get to work, struggling to function when I was there.

Life took on a nightmarish quality. It seemed to be permanently dark. The dense black of the night on the way to work, barely punctuated by streetlights. The shaded clamour of words in the badly lit pub as I floundered around behind the bar. Even the faces crowded up to the bar, closing me in as I attempted to work, seemed to be shrouded. After work, I faced the lonely drive home in my old black car, back to my cold, empty flat. I worried endlessly about how I could afford to buy food, pay the bills and the rent. Not to mention paying for the fags and the drink and the dope.

My friend Claire had her own problems, and returned to her mother's home in Bristol to try to work them out. I was more alone than ever.

I did have company, in the form of a German Shepherd dog I'd bought when I was working at the Royal Bath. One of the croupiers had bred a litter, and I decided that I needed a dog in the flat to protect me. I christened him Ben, and I loved him deeply.

But Ben did not return my love. He was hard work. I had picked the biggest and strongest pup in the litter, and he was determined to be the leader of our two-person pack. Ben was not soft and cuddly for more than a few days. He never obeyed my commands, he thought nothing of nipping me to keep me in my place, and his teeth were as sharp as little razors. My clothes and my nerves were soon reduced to shreds.

I stopped going to work. I forgot to eat. I stayed up all night alone in my flat, chain smoking and drinking herbal tea. I had a copy of Rudyard Kipling's book 'Kim', and managed to read all sorts of implications and mathematical equations into it, as well as receiving the 'message' that it was time for me to go off on my travels.

And travel I did, in an ambulance to St Ann's Hospital again, via the police station. It was Easter 1994, exactly six years after my first breakdown. I burned with confusion and humiliation on the way to the hospital because I was restrained in a straitjacket, although I had never in my life been violent towards any person, animal or object.

46

St Ann's, Again

I soon discovered that the quality of life inside a mental hospital had not improved in the years since I was last there. Thinking back to it now, the memories of that second hospitalisation merge with the first. The worst part of both was the same, being forced to take medication, physically pinned down while I was injected with various chemical substances. It was gratuitous brutality disguised as treatment.

I was told that I was in Merlin Ward, although I had no idea of the distinction between one ward and another. They told me I was seriously ill and that this was an acute ward, but I found it hard to believe that anybody who was in St Ann's was not acutely ill, was not desperate. This was not a place where anyone would want to be if they had any sort of choice. The ward was mixed, male and female, all age groups.

I clung to a brochure that I had brought with me to hospital. During the time when I was disintegrating emotionally, somebody had offered me the opportunity to be a salesperson for Dorling Kindersley, the publishing company. It was a direct marketing position; I would sell a range of children's books either from my home or other peoples', and receive commission on the sales. I was in so much emotional turmoil that I never held a single book party. But still I clung to the brochure, which signalled to me the promise of a new life, a career.

Another woman, Betty, was after my brochure. She was twice my age, and she was determined to part me from my precious book. Whenever she got the chance, she crept up, grabbed it from me and cooed over it. 'It's mine!' she would cackle. She did this whenever she got the chance, and the brochure soon became torn and ratty and no longer looked like the promise of a new life.

I knew that Betty was deliberately winding me up and that I shouldn't react, but her behaviour still angered me. Most of the anger came from fear. I recognised this woman, and some of the other patients, from the last time I was here. I was scared that, like Betty and the others, I would end up in and out of this institution for years, or permanently inside it. I was terrified at the prospect.

Betty never left me alone. She pointed out a male nurse and told me that he had raped her. 'He has been coming to my room every night for years now and raping me.' I shunned her and her miserable stories. I didn't believe her for a second and I didn't want to listen to her nonsense. Why would anybody want to rape a mad old woman? Betty told everybody her story, and nobody else believed it either.

Once I had settled down, I played by the rules, took the medication and never confided anything of what I thought or felt to any of the nursing staff. Visitors came and went, usually my sisters and my mother. Once, two of the girls I worked with at Stanley's casino came to visit. I felt humiliated that they should see me in this state, and I barely spoke to them. I was grateful that I had not been forgotten by my family and friends, but I was unsettled after their visits. Still, the time passed and nothing awful happened. Then again, everything awful happened, but I still somehow survived the six weeks or so until I was allowed to leave the hospital.

I was not better, not at all. I went back to my flat

but I was a nervous wreck, slow from all the drugs and very scared. What had I become, I wondered? And what would become of me?

I had brought home a supply of medication which I was told to take at regular intervals throughout the day. My mother had visited me nearly every day in St Ann's, but now she backed off. She was still working at the same hospital, which had been relocated to newly built premises and re-named the Royal Bournemouth Hospital. She was busy.

I, on the other hand, had nothing to do. Nothing whatsoever. I was not smoking now, I had stopped in hospital again, so I couldn't even do that. After a couple of weeks of complete inactivity, I was visited by a community psychiatric nurse. She asked me what I wanted out of life now that I was out of hospital. I said that I wanted something to do, and friends to spend time with. She referred me to a day hospital, Hahnemann House in Bournemouth town centre. Here, it was intended that I would build up my confidence and learn to become a worthwhile member of society again.

47

Hahnemann House

At least I was able to stop worrying about how I would physically survive. I was receiving benefits, and my rent was paid by the council. I had stopped smoking and couldn't drink because of the medication I was taking, and anyway I was too embarrassed to meet up with any of my old friends. All this meant that I lived live cleanly, and cheaply. I was even given a free hot lunch, at the day hospital.

I attended Hanhemann House for around a month before I began to hope that things might improve. There was no pressure here. The nursing staff tried to educate the patients about mental illness, and made some half-hearted attempts to motivate us into activity, but most of the time we were left alone. I felt safe and relaxed.

One day, everything changed. The doctors called me in for a meeting, with my mother. There were at least six people in the room, nurses and doctors of various rank. They all looked serious when they broke the bombshell. I had schizophrenia, they told me. I was schizophrenic.

This information had already been on my medical records for six years, they said. I'd been diagnosed when I was nineteen, at the time of my first breakdown, but it was not thought appropriate to inform me at the time.

It was a lot to take on board. For the six years since my first breakdown, I had considered myself to be normal. Nervous, extremely nervous, but essentially normal. In this period of time I had completed my degree, held down various jobs and relationships, and functioned in society. I had often struggled but despite two long stays in St Ann's Hospital, my life to date had been, more or less, a success. Now anything I had achieved was thrown into doubt, because all this time I'd been living with a disabling illness. These people had known about it all along and I had confirmed their belief by breaking down again.

I remember my mother turning to me when we left the room. 'I don't think you have that,' she said. I disregarded her. I held the medical profession in high regard, I trusted doctors, and couldn't see any reason why they would break such earth-shattering news unless they were completely sure of their diagnosis.

I was terrified. I was convinced that this diagnosis meant I was a freak, a social outcast. An unknown quantity. A maniac. After all, I was a schizophrenic. I was hardly human. I would never have judged others this harshly, but I was unremittingly cruel in my assessment of myself.

The 'Team' told me later that the prognosis was bad and when I asked what a prognosis was, they said that it meant I would get worse as I grew older. I could never expect to be normal, and this was something I had to accept. I must face the fact that I had no future.

I lost all hope. My only comfort was in the medication they prescribed. I still didn't like taking drugs, but they made me comfortably numb. I walked around in an induced stupor, so at least I wasn't panicking, but they affected my mind and body so much that every simple action or interaction became an effort.

I decided it wasn't worth making that effort. I switched off mentally, receded into a trance-like state and refused to take any part in what was going on around me. That was easily done at Hanhemann House, since nobody seemed to expect anything of me anyway. I could drift through the days lazily, lounging around half-asleep on the various saggy, stained sofas provided for the purpose. I started smoking again because all the other patients did, and because it seemed as reasonable a way to pass the time as any other.

Occasionally, I attended one of the rehabilitative talks that were supposed to be the primary reason for being at Hahnemann House, but nothing much was expected in the way of participation. I sat in my chair, eyes half-open, then eyelids drooping...closing...

I must have been paying attention in at least one of these talks, because I learned that schizophrenia affected one per cent of the population. I was also taught that schizophrenics were not aggressive, and in fact were far more likely to hurt themselves than other people. But nothing distracted me from the fear that the word schizophrenia struck into my heart, and the prognosis I had been given. I felt that my life was effectively over, and nobody could have convinced me otherwise.

I sold my old, beloved Morris Minor, into which my brother had fitted a new engine. I decided I didn't need to drive any more, since I was going nowhere. I was also relieved of responsibility for my dog. My brother Stephen had looked after Ben while I was in hospital and by the time I got out three months later, he had grown so huge and was so far out of control that I told Steve he could keep him. Steve was delighted, but I felt even more of a failure. Now I had nothing of worth or note in my life. I was convinced I didn't deserve anything good anyway.

I returned from the day hospital to my flat one afternoon, to discover that it had been burgled. I was

224

surprised by how vulnerable this made me feel. I told myself I had become weak, and easily impressionable. My sister Mandy, who was now back to England, urged me to give up my flat and move in with her.

It was a mistake. For one thing, there was no space for me. I had to sleep on the floor of her small daughter's bedroom. Also, my sister refused to accept my assessment of myself and my lack of enthusiasm for life. She nagged me relentlessly, trying to make me go to the gym, socialise more. I resented this. Mandy had no concept of what I was going through, she couldn't possibly understand how it felt to be labelled as I was.

Before the burglary, I had been unhappy but relatively comfortable. I had been attending the day hospital for eighteen months. My days started slowly. I'd stay in bed until midday then catch the bus to Hanhemann House, where I'd have my free lunch then spend the afternoon smoking and watching TV. I had become well upholstered from these lunches. I ate a three-course meal every day, with second helpings. In my defence, the medications I was taking made me very hungry.

Mandy tried to shake me out of these comfortable, but damaging, habits. She bought me a car for a few hundred pounds and instructed me to take her daughter to nursery school and collect her, and run other errands. She made me do my share of cleaning around the house. In other words, she tried to make me useful.

I did whatever my sister asked, but took no interest in any of it, refusing to muster any enthusiasm. I did not want to be involved in the world at any level, or to have to explain myself. I did my best not to intrude on Mandy's life and in return I asked only to be left alone. I couldn't comprehend why my sister found this so difficult to do.

I had effectively disappeared as far as most of my friends were concerned, although Mandy's home was only a few miles away from my old flat. My friend Louise from the kibbutz surprised me one day. She was in Bournemouth visiting her father, somehow found out where I was living and pitched up at the door. We spent a day together. I was grateful to Louise for believing I was worth bothering with but I knew I was a shadow of the friend she had once known. There was no joy left in me. I was only a schizophrenic.

Mandy kept on nagging. She made me join the gym, but I only went when she took me and did the minimum amount of exercise I could get away with. And I kept on eating excessively, all the meals she provided, the big lunches at the day hospital, crisps and sweets from the local shop. The junk food had a mildly numbing effect on my mind and I felt they helped my body to look the way I felt inside, blubbery and helpless. Maybe the outside world would finally leave me alone, I thought, as I got bigger and bigger.

After about six months of sharing her home with me, my sister lost her temper one evening. She was raging and shouting and the anger in her eyes made me shrivel inside, but I had no idea what I had done wrong because I could not hear a single word she was saying. I'd gone completely deaf. I could only see her mouth opening and closing and those furious eyes drilling into my soul.

It seemed to last for ages and was the strangest sensation, not being able to hear a word but watching my sister rage at me. I felt detached, floaty, although I was a little concerned about whether my hearing would ever return. It occurred to me that the deafness would have come in useful when I was young and defenceless in the face of my father's wrath. My mind began to drift. I realised that my sister did not know that I was deaf and that nothing I could have said would have reached her anyway when she was in this state. Then my hearing returned as suddenly as it had gone. 'Get out!' Mandy was screaming at me. 'Get out!'

I was shaking. Where could I go, I wondered? It didn't matter. I found a bag, a black dustbin liner, and began to pack my possessions. I didn't have any money. My social security payments were tiny now that I didn't have a home of my own, and most of the money went to my sister for housekeeping.

But I didn't object. I was in shock, and I only wanted to get out of my sister's sight. I put the bin liner into my car. My sister followed me outside, shouting at me in front of all the neighbours, insisting that I left my door key. I took it out of my bag, went back into the house and put it down on the coffee table. I wouldn't look at my sister or speak to her, in case she started the shouting again. I was utterly confused as I drove off in my car, with no idea of where I was heading. The thin, inadequate bubble that had protected me whilst stealing any autonomy I still possessed, had burst. I was as naked and vulnerable as a baby.

48
The YMCA

I was now homeless. I was also about four stone too heavy, and stuck in an extremely deep rut. But for some time now there had been more going on between my ears than anyone would have guessed from my vacant façade. I had chosen not to participate in the world and hadn't spent any effort on anything for some time, but my thoughts were no longer disordered. The lingering apathy and lack of confidence were not exactly an act, but I knew that I was not as ill as the staff at Hahnemann House believed. I had not got as far as questioning the diagnosis. I still believed that the experts knew more about my state of mind than I understood myself.

I wondered what to do. It was late, about nine o'clock in the evening. I went to the only place that I thought might help me. Hanhemann House. There was always someone on duty at night because it had a few long-term residents as well as the day patients. The nurse on duty was concerned but said I could not stay there because I was not a medical priority. He directed me instead to a night shelter for the homeless.

At the shelter, I was given a bed with the minimum of fuss. The staff there were used to desperate people arriving in various guises at all hours of the night and were not at all fazed. But by the following morning I was desperate to leave. I'd been awake all night, terrified by the other occupants of the room where I had been supposed to sleep. It was as bad as being in St Ann's.

Because I had no choice, I was making more of an effort to look after myself than I had done for some time. I showered early in the morning and left the night shelter before anyone else was up. I had formulated a plan. I was going to ask for a room at the YMCA in Bournemouth town centre.

My friend Claire from the Royal Bath Casino had lived in a proper flat within the YMCA, but I knew from her that the hostel was open to anybody who needed a place to stay. Claire had stayed at the YMCA on a self-catering basis but there was a communal dining room where most residents ate.

At first this suited me. I had my own room and the staff at the 'Y' made everything easy, helping me fill out the forms for benefits to pay the rent and informing me exactly how much I would have to contribute towards meals.

The other residents scared me. They were almost all male, loud and aggressive, and they pursued anyone with any semblance of femininity, including me. I was dismayed. I had worked so hard to become invisible, but in the YMCA no woman was allowed to be an island.

I feared the dining room particularly. The moment any woman entered there was a hush, a lot of staring and sniggering and then the room went quiet again but the staring became more intense. The experience was mortifying every time.

The dining room was the only common area of the Y that I couldn't avoid entirely. There was also the fact that I had paid for the food and it was plentiful and tasty. I began to avoid it, though, unless I was very hungry. Even then, I went in, ate as quickly as possible, and promptly left again.

We had to vacate our rooms at the YMCA early in the mornings and I didn't want to go straight to Hahnemann House so I decided to take up swimming again as a way to pass the time. I also gave up smoking once more, because being able to breathe more freely made the swimming easier.

During the six months I stayed with Mandy, I had begun to see one of my old friends, Mark Lee. Mark was a little younger than me, about my height, thin and wiry, with a Fifties hairstyle and an extensive knowledge of everything from that era, especially music and cars. He sang a lot, often while he was driving. He had a good voice for speaking as well as singing. His deep, cultured tones were at odds with his rather shabby appearance.

Mark was a bit of an oddity. I had known him for a long time and was aware that he fancied me. I had never found him at all attractive and I still didn't, but his company was undemanding, and I never felt that he judged me. Mark found me at the YMCA and we started to go to the cinema together on Friday nights, and for coffee and ice cream afterwards. His presence was useful because it made the YMCA lads keep their distance. They thought I had a boyfriend.

I spent seven tortuous weeks at the YMCA before one of the receptionists at Hanhemann House beckoned me over one morning. I liked Pat. She was kind, motherly. She was one of the few members of staff at Hahnemann who I spoke to regularly, so she knew that I was no longer living with my sister. I had no idea that her husband was the general manager of Bournemouth Churches Housing Association or that BCHA was building a new block of flats.

It came as a complete shock when Pat asked if I would be interested in applying for one of these flats. I certainly was, and I immediately went for an interview

230

with her husband Peter. Thank goodness, he approved of me. I was in. I couldn't believe my luck. I had brand-new, low-cost housing. It was the perfect opportunity to make a fresh start.

I moved into my new home a short time later, in September 1995. It was on the second floor of a block called Henley Court, near the centre of Bournemouth. It had a kitchen, lounge-diner, bedroom and bathroom. It was carpeted and had curtains. All of it was new and all of it was perfection, especially after the way I had been living.

Sadly, at this crucial moment, I succumbed to cowardice. I had a home of my own, but I was scared to be there alone. This felt stupid, because the place was secure, but I felt vulnerable. So I clung to Mark. I agreed to be his girlfriend within a month of moving into my new flat.

I tried hard to love Mark. I convinced myself that he needed looking after and nurturing and that by caring for him I could make him into the sort of person I could be comfortable loving. But once more, I had ignored the only advice my mother ever gave me, to 'Be True Unto Yourself'. Once again, I had a boyfriend, a champion and protector. Somebody I could hide behind.

49
Goodbye, Dad

In January 1997, my father passed away. He never met Mark.

Dad died in terrible circumstances. He had been disabled by an accident and after being bedridden for more than a year, was diagnosed with cancer. The tumours were in his stomach and his lungs. He must have been in awful pain for some time.

He was the father of nine children, but my sister Jane was the only one who visited him regularly towards the end of his life. I only went with her once. I was upset to see him so unwell, but his spirit was still indomitable, and Jane and I couldn't help smiling as we watched him place telephone bets to the bookmaker as he lay prone in bed.

At this time, Dad lived in a council flat. It was squalid and practically unfurnished, although he had lived there for around five years. There was no sofa, table or anything you would expect to find in a home. It was not even carpeted.

Dad had been provided with a home help who cleaned occasionally. He had 'meals on wheels' delivered. Because he was bedridden he also qualified for some basic help with his physical needs. It was strange to think of him being cared for by strangers, although this rudimentary servicing barely qualified as care. The thing that struck me, or perhaps just strikes me now with hindsight, is that he never complained about his lot. In fact, he never had. I never heard him regret the lack of friendship in his life, or mention the fact that his large family failed to look after him.

Dad talked a lot about money, and had plenty of illusions that he had been done down on that account. But he never bemoaned the lack of love in his life. Perhaps he didn't expect to be loved. Perhaps he didn't feel that he deserved it. This theory would fit with the little I knew about his own background, that he was sent to boarding school at the age of seven, at a time when male boarding schools were brutal places. I think that probably my father knew deep loneliness, but he never once admitted to it.

At least my mother was there at the end of his life. She had recently taken voluntary redundancy from her hospital job and found work as a Matron in a nursing home. When she discovered how ill Dad was, she arranged for him to be taken to her place of work.

I felt numb and helpless in the days leading to my father's death. I visited the nursing home regularly, bought him pyjamas and razors. He owned literally nothing at that stage. He asked me to buy him lottery tickets, told me the numbers he had chosen and I wrote them down. My Dad was on his death bed, and he still wanted to play the lottery. My brain could not cope with this.

A visiting GP cornered me in the corridor. He seemed perturbed by my apparent lack of emotion. 'You do realise, Louise, that your father is about to die?' he asked. I knew he wanted tears, evidence of my humanity. I looked at him, this simple doctor. If I had words to express how I felt, I would have told him that he knew nothing about my life, about my feelings. 'This is the man who told me I was a prostitute when I was thirteen years old,' I would have said. 'Yes, this is the man who gave me life. But he is also the man I saw spitting at my mother in the street. How do you think you would feel now, if you were me?' I said nothing, of course, just nodded in acknowledgement of his question, keeping my eyes carefully dead.

My father was only resident in the nursing home for a few days before he passed away. Mum was at Dad's side when he drew his last breath, in January 1997. He was 77.

Dad had expressed a wish for a traditional Jewish burial. In fact, he had paid for it in advance. My mother was present at that service, along with five of his children, including myself. The Rabbi was diplomatic at the burial service. Without praising my father, he managed to impart a sense of loss at the demise of a worthwhile person.

My sisters and I were grateful that the Rabbi was kind and we thanked him afterwards for his tact and diplomacy. 'I liked Leslie' he said. I was puzzled. Could this be true? I filed it mentally for future reference, along with the testimony of my friend Claire from the Royal Bath, and the cashier there, Adam. The Rabbi suggested that someone should write a book about my father's life. He was looking straight at me as he said this. I turned my head away.

It is a strange paradox that childhood experiences can haunt people until they are long into adulthood, and often leave scars that last forever. It took years after my father's death before I began to realise that he was, after all, a human being.

Gradually, I started to build a fuller picture of him. I no longer felt pure dislike or fear. I was a long way from canonising his memory. My childhood still haunted me too much for that. But I tried to understand him, and began to realise that any person's life is a complicated process, and nobody is all good or all bad. It was the first step towards forgiveness, and my reward was to feel a little better in myself. Forgiveness, in the end, is essential to recovery. Once I knew that I couldn't simultaneously hate my father and love myself, I was finally ready to heal.

50

Tick-Tock

For the first year of our relationship, Mark came to my flat for dinner and then spent the night, but didn't share any of the living expenses and continued to pay rent for the room in the shared house that was his official abode.

I was irritated that Mark didn't want to commit to the relationship and this made me contrary minded. I persuaded him to move in properly. He was working hard, having set up a business with a like-minded friend, buying and selling cars from a small yard. The smell of oil hung over him permanently.

Before long they expanded to a bigger yard, with more second-hand cars for sale, and over the next few years the business went from strength to strength until it had several employees and a considerable turnover.

The years passed. Our lifestyle was very low key. There was little of interest or excitement, which suited me. I didn't need a social life. I did see one friend, Claire from the Royal Bath Casino, who had returned to Bournemouth with her son Tom. She and her husband Alan had another child together, who they named Louise. I spent as much time with Claire as possible, not only because she was my only friend, but also because I doted on her baby.

I also wrote to some old friends from Israel; Louise, a kibbutznik called Renana, and Dalia and Ramy, my 'adoptive parents'. Dalia never failed to reply to my letters.

Another friend from the kibbutz, my room-mate Clare, who had pitched up in Southampton while I was at uni there, also kept in touch. She lived in New

Zealand now with Paul, and I was surprised when she wrote to tell me they were returning to England for their wedding. I was touched and honoured when she asked me to be a bridesmaid and I agreed, although I was terrified at the prospect of a high profile, public role.

Events snowballed. Time passed too quickly and all too soon I found myself shivering outside a picture postcard church in Hampshire for Clare and Paul's January wedding. I did my best to carry out the duties of a bridesmaid but remained blank in my emotions and outlook. Although my last breakdown had been years earlier, I still took psychiatric medication, risperidone, for 'prophylactic reasons'. I was told, and I believed, that I would become ill if I did not. My head felt as if it was permanently stuffed full of cotton wool.

 I did not make a vivacious bridesmaid. It was lucky that Clare had a maid of honour too, her brother's wife, who was more awake than me and consequently a lot more helpful.

Mark became embedded in his career, and the accumulation of money. I worked too, in a series of menial jobs, chambermaiding in hotels. I spent three years at one of these, the Manor House Hotel on the East Cliff of Bournemouth.

 Joan and her husband Terry, who owned the hotel, were Londoners. I liked them both. They were kind, if a little volatile. I took to the work too. I didn't enjoy cleaning particularly, but I liked the fact that I could work at my own pace, potter from room to room, and listen to the radio as I worked. Also, the work kept me fit. I had lost all the weight I gained after I was in St Ann's, and it was important to me to keep it off.

237

The only radio station that the hotel bedrooms tuned into was Radio Two, and luckily Golden Oldies and easy listening classics were just my thing. I had never been sophisticated in my musical tastes.

I got along reasonably well with the other chambermaids although I didn't make any great friends at work as I had in the past. Some days I stayed at the hotel into the afternoons, working on the reception desk. Reception was quiet, which suited me as I could read magazines or sit and daydream while I was there. It also gave me a chance to pursue my new hobby. I had finally taken steps to put my dream into action and was trying to become a writer.

I had always dreamt of writing, but since my last incarceration in hospital I had put these dreams behind me. It scared me to think back to when I was unhinged, out of control, running hell-for-leather from St Ann's shouting, 'I am a writer!' The fact that I had finally admitted again that writing was what I wanted to do, and was moving towards it, was a massive step forward psychologically.

I enrolled in a creative writing class. I knew I didn't need lessons, I only needed to write as much as possible and learn as I went along. But the classes gave me encouragement. The other students praised my work from the first occasion when I read aloud in class, and I got a real kick from this. Of course, they praised everybody's work; it was one of the pre-requisites of being in a writing class. But still.

Because I had lived a low-key existence for so long, and because I was still taking anti-psychotic medication (anti-psychotics are basically major tranquillisers) I found I could cope with the classroom environment at first. My sensitivity had lessened, and I was grateful for this. However, after about a term of classes, my old fears about blushing, and the blushing itself, started to creep back. I stuck with the classes for another year, although I was finding them tortuous, because I was determined to become a writer.

I invested a couple of hundred pounds in a second-hand computer. The only practical way to write now was to use a word processor. I didn't know where to start at first, because I had never used a computer at school, and only once or twice at university. So I enrolled in more evening classes, working towards the RSA exams in word processing. I reasoned that if I never became a writer, I would at least be qualified as a secretary.

Once I had learned to use my computer, I used it a lot. I wrote my diary each day, endless boring liturgies about how I had spent my time, how much I had eaten, how much I weighed, who I had seen and spoken to, what time Mark came home in the evening. Reading them over was like watching paint dry, only worse. It was a good thing that I did not yet embark on any creative writing except my homework from the evening classes. My brain was definitely not in gear.

I was starting to tire of my day job. Years of cleaning for a living had left me exhausted. I spent my days cleaning up other peoples' messes. My education had equipped me for something better, I decided. I wanted to be proud of myself. I knew I wasn't ready to make a living from writing, and I doubted my ability to get a better job than chambermaiding, but I had started to consider the possibility at least.

I fitted in another job around my hotel work. This was as cleaner for an elderly gentleman who lived alone in a large house in a select area of Bournemouth. He had been married twice, had grown-up children, and was an intelligent and interesting man. I enjoyed talking to him. I had a key to his house but he was usually at home when I went in to clean, and we would chat over coffee during my morning break.

Mr Button took me seriously. He knew nothing of my breakdowns, and he could never make sense of the fact that I had a degree in law and yet worked as a cleaner. He didn't realise how socially inept I was, because he only saw me on a one-to-one basis and I functioned reasonably well in those circumstances. I talked to him about my writing ambitions and he encouraged me, and gradually over the years he gave me the courage to believe that I was cut out for better things in life than I had become accustomed to.

Back at home, my relationship with Mark had gone from bad to worse. Our arguments became more regular and bitter. Mark had never hurried back from work but he began to come home so late, and so tired, that we spent no time at all together. We argued about the same subjects, over and over.

We were fundamentally unsuited. One evening, Mark came home from work when I was busy cleaning the flat. I was hot and tired, my hair was tied back into a rough ponytail. He stared at me in delight. 'You've done your hair!' he said.

I wondered what on earth he was talking about. I realised only when I went to check my appearance in the mirror. I had pinned my fringe back with a hair clip, but it had slipped forwards into a quiff, a simulacrum of a Fifties hairstyle. I was horrified. The man I lived with was a stranger, a complete mystery to me, and he thought I was trying to please him by adopting a hairstyle that imitated his own.

Our relationship was massively dysfunctional. We were both obviously unhappy. As time went on, I lost sight of Mark's good points and could only see the things about him that drove me crazy. But I still clung to the hope that matters would improve. The reason was simple. I wanted a child.

As the years passed, my biological clock had become imperious. I must procreate, I believed. It was an imperative. I also believed that Mark represented my only chance to become a parent. I had invested so much time already in this relationship that it simply had to work. I was aware that Mark did not want a child but I was sure that he would love our baby when it arrived.

Mark claimed he believed it was wrong to have a child without being married and he was sure I wouldn't agree to marry him. I didn't need to think about it. 'All right,' I said, like a stubborn donkey set on a carrot. (I was the donkey and the baby was the carrot.) 'All right. Let's get married.' It was clear from Mark's expression that he hadn't bargained for this. He would lose face if he backed down though. And, although I was horrified at what was happening, that I was planning to marry someone with whom I was permanently at loggerheads, I stood firm too.

Soon we become embroiled in all sorts of complicated plans and arrangements involving outfits, invitations and other nonsense. The heralded day approached quicker than I would ever have believed possible, and suddenly in front of me loomed the prospect of making a public and legally binding commitment to a relationship so full of holes that it was practically transparent.

51
A Wedding

As our wedding day approached, I got progressively closer to calling the whole thing off. What stopped me was the fact that, poor as our relationship was, I felt he was all I had. And vice versa, I suppose. I still phoned my mother and sisters regularly, but I didn't often see any of them, since they were all busy with their own affairs. I still had friends in theory, but none of them lived close by, or weren't tied up in their own relationships.

Apart from Claire, the only group I went out with socially in Bournemouth had been Dave's friends from my teenage years, when he and I lived together. Now that I was no longer jealous of them, I enjoyed their company and found it preferable to being alone. But the problem I had in any group was that I became excessively self-conscious, and to combat my awkwardness I drank or smoked dope and neither of these courses of action benefitted my mental health.

I realised it was better for me, health wise, to be socially reclusive. This was how I had become so dependent on Mark. I knew that he cared about me. Also, I was broody. I was sure I would get on better with Mark once I had a baby to love and look after. I would be happier and calmer, and this would make everything easier.

There were other people involved in our wedding plans. Mark's parents and sisters and my own family and friends were all excited, waiting eagerly for our big day. My niece Yasmin was beside herself at the thought of being my bridesmaid. I did not want to humiliate Mark by cancelling the wedding, and I did not dare to consider how alone I would be without him and without that dearly anticipated child.

On the day before the wedding, I still wasn't sure whether I would go through with it. Of course, I did. I was that much of an idiot. I spent the whole ceremony encased in a fuzz of panic, and for the whole of the party afterwards I felt vacant and bemused.

The reception party was a disco at the Queen's Park Club in Bournemouth. I had first joined the club at Mandy's insistence when I shared her home, but soon stopped going. I'd rejoined when I moved into Henley Court, and four years later I was one of the most regular attendees at the re-named Fitness First Club. I had nothing to do with the other members socially, but I was there every day, rain or shine, plodding up and down the swimming pool. I found that swimming, like writing my diary, alleviated stress.

Some of my old friends came to the wedding, and I felt grateful to them for supporting me. Afterwards, Mark and I went home to sleep, and the next day we headed off to honeymoon in Torquay for a week. And then life continued as usual.

Except for one crucial factor. We were now officially trying for a baby! The months passed and there was no sign of a pregnancy. I could not fathom it.

By what seemed like a stroke of fate, I chanced upon a magazine article that explained matters. The doctors at Hanhemann House had assured me that the medication I had been taking for four years in no way affected my chances of having a baby. They also said it was safe to conceive while on the drug. But this small paragraph in Health and Fitness magazine suggested otherwise. The drug I was on, I discovered, might have been altering my hormone levels, meaning I had no chance at all of conceiving.

My GP raised his eyebrows when I suggested to him that I thought I had raised prolactin levels. He affected not to know what I was talking about, but he sent me off with a slip to have the appropriate blood tests. When I returned to his office a week later, he looked at me differently. It was a look I had never seen from a GP before. Respect. 'Your prolactin levels are sky high,' he said, and immediately referred me to see an endocrinologist at Poole Hospital.

The consultant put me on a programme of hormone therapy, which amounted to fertility treatment. She also authorised me to stop taking the psychiatric medication that was preventing me from conceiving. I was confused again, sensing that the medical professionals I trusted had betrayed me. I had never doubted anything that they told me. But it was now obvious that I had been deliberately deceived.

The psychiatrists at Hanhemann House had said that the medication I took posed no problems for conception. I had believed them without question and might have carried on trying to conceive indefinitely if I hadn't found out the truth for myself. I sensed now that there was some sort of conspiracy, an unspoken one, to stop me, and others who had been mentally ill, from having children. I felt puzzled and bitter about this. But at least I was now on the right track, with the fertility treatment.

There was another problem. It became obvious that Mark did not want a baby at all and that I was forcing him to fit in with my dream. I did eventually get pregnant, briefly, but after a few weeks I miscarried. I was devastated, but Mark showed no concern at all.

I had a moment of clarity. The relationship was hopeless and I needed to leave it. Mark and I went to marriage counselling, where the counsellor listened to our story then summed it up. He suggested to Mark that I had been a bird with a broken wing and he had nursed me back to health. Perhaps, said the counsellor, now that I was better, he should let me fly away. Mark disagreed, saying that we were meant for each other and had always been so. I privately thought that the counsellor had a point, but I said nothing.

When we emerged from the counsellor's office my husband and I looked at one another and dissolved into laughter. We laughed so hard we nearly wet ourselves. I was laughing because the whole situation was so ridiculous, and so hopeless. I had no idea what Mark found so funny. We laughed until we cried, and the counsellor looked out from an upstairs window to see us in paroxysms.

No amount of counselling could salvage this wreck, and after six sessions we agreed to lay our marriage to rest. I was deeply despondent. My marriage was dead. Far worse, so was my baby.

But I still suffered from the same old fear, the terror of being alone. Mark's presence was exasperating and I frequently asked him to leave the flat, but his absence made me desperate too. Every time he left, I asked him to return. Even a holiday I had planned to get away from it all (Mr Button gave me the free use of his time-share apartment in Tenerife for a week) somehow turned into a holiday with Mark, a miserable experience for both of us.

During our fourth or fifth 'separation', I realised that the marriage would never be truly over until I found another partner to replace Mark. This seemed an impossibility. I was not attracted to other men. I'd been going to the gym every day for five years and had never seen anyone there who took my fancy. How on earth could I expect to meet anyone? How, and where, and why should it happen?

I was in despair. What would become of me? Where could I turn? How could I keep on, year after year, making a mess of my life, over and over? I was convinced that this time I was completely sunk, and I was ready to surrender.

52
Another Funeral

I had no idea that I was on the verge of turning a corner in my life. It was 1999 and I was thirty years old. Now that I had stopped taking the psychiatric drugs that had sedated me for so long, I felt as if I was starting to wake up. I wanted more out of life than I had wanted for many years. I wanted to participate in it properly. But I needed a serious attitude change in order for this to happen.

I had unhappy news at around this time. An old friend, one of the group of people I'd hung out with in Bournemoutth as a teenager, died tragically young, due to addiction. I saw some of the old crowd at his funeral and we were all devastated by the loss. He was not the only one of the group to have died prematurely. Another chap had recently come to a grim end in a road traffic accident. Additional casualties included more people with long-term addiction problems. There were too many lost lives.

There could be no doubt that our group were paying the price of youthful overindulgence. There were some recovery stories, like one friend who was married with two children and living in Scotland, well away from the peer group who had led him into temptation. Some of the others had grown up and were leading more restrained lives. They had perhaps not over-indulged as heavily as the rest of us, or maybe they coped better with excess.

But most of my erstwhile friends were in a bad way. I did not want to be one of those paying the final toll. There was addiction in my blood. I had a gambler for a father, an alcoholic mother. I knew that in order to survive, I needed to live a 'clean' life. On the other hand, I didn't want to live at half pace any longer. I knew I was not a person who could journey through life alone, that I needed support. I needed a relationship to keep me steady. But to make any real headway in my life I would have to start being more honest and open about my own needs and, crucially, never again settle for anyone less than the right person.

I spoke regularly on the telephone to my friend Louise from the kibbutz. She had lived abroad for many years but had recently returned to England. Louise was a calm and sensible source of advice, and I often confided in her about my problems.

I was still going to the gym regularly, and Louise was horrified to learn that I was still wearing my wedding ring on my trips there. She insisted that I should take it off, on the grounds that my marriage was over and I would never meet anyone new if I wore this 'disguise'. She also advised me to be friendlier at the gym, because even if I didn't meet a man I liked I would feel less lonely.

I had a new job. For the first time in my life, I was working in an office, a call centre in the headquarters of a large insurance company. I had left the health section blank on the application form, because I knew I would not get the job if I was honest about my mental health history. Why should I have to tell anybody these personal details? I got on well at work, fitted into the environment and gelled with my fellow employees. Soon after I started work, I wrote a short article for the company magazine, which got noticed by the management, and consequently I was commissioned to work on an in-house newsletter.

All this made me feel that I was on the way to

fulfilling my writing ambitions. This was compounded by the fact that I was doing some paid writing work, on a local magazine, 'Viewpoint'. The editor was a fellow student from my writing class and she had asked me to work for her on a freelance basis. I became the official motoring correspondent for her magazine, and also wrote general articles and did some interviews. It was poorly paid but I didn't care. I loved seeing my name in print, and would happily have paid the magazine for that privilege.

A lot of things in my life had changed in the few months since I'd split up from Mark. My marriage was over but at least I had found the courage to admit it and to let Mark and myself off the hook of a hopeless predicament. We had been so diametrically opposed in our attitudes and outlooks from the beginning that the marriage could never have succeeded. Now he could get on with making a new life and, hopefully, eventually find someone who suited him better than me. I bore him no malice and I hoped he felt the same way.

53
Paul

I was going through changes. I was holding down a decent job, and the prospect of a career in writing beckoned promisingly. I had made some new friends at work and was socialising more at the gym too. I met a lad called Steve one evening in the swimming pool and after getting changed I went to speak to him in the bar. Then I noticed the man with him. Steve introduced us. Paul grinned at me. And I fell for him.

Before that June day in 1999, I would have said that love at first sight was possible in theory, but not as a working reality. For example, I'd been smitten when I had met Alexander at Kibbutz Revivim, but that turned out to be a mere crush, which gradually receded into distant memory.

This was different. When Paul smiled at me that evening, I felt that I was home. Neither of us said much. I sensed it was right for me to be with him, and that he felt the same way too.

A couple of nights later, Paul took me to a local pub, where we sat and drink beer in the garden, watching the ducks swim downstream past us. We talked a little, laughed a lot. It was perfect. Before long, I had introduced him to my family. Jane was concerned. She quizzed me, as only a sister would have the nerve to, about what contraceptives I was using, and was astounded when I told her I wasn't using any. Did I not know the risks, she asked.

Well, durr! We were both adults, both aware of the consequences of our actions, and both happy to accept them as they came. We were in love!

The divorce from Mark came through rapidly. We had no children and we had separate bank accounts, so there were no financial issues to be resolved. The flat was in my name and was only rented anyway. The furniture and all the contents were mine. It was as straightforward as any divorce could have been. I saved the cost of a lawyer by filling out all the necessary forms myself and filing them in person at the court.

The grounds for divorce were a slight problem. The most dignified way would have been two years' separation, but I didn't want to wait that long. Another option would be to claim 'unreasonable behaviour' by one or both of us. But these grounds would need to be laid out in detail, involving a certain amount of muck-raking, which I didn't want to do either.

Instead, I wrote on the divorce forms that I had committed adultery. Which I technically did, since I was still married when I met Paul, but not in the deceitful and underhand way that the word implies, because Mark and I were separated at the time. It sped up the divorce, landing all the unpleasantness and blame at my door, which I accepted because I felt guilty about leaving Mark and moving on so swiftly.

Mark and I had lived together for about three years before our marriage but were married for just over a year and separated for half of that time. The divorce took only six weeks to be finalised. In some ways, it felt as if the marriage had never happened.

In July 1999, a few weeks into my relationship with Paul, I went on a writers' holiday at the prestigious Arvon Centre in Devon. I had booked and paid for it months before, and had eagerly anticipated it, but now that I had met Paul I didn't want to leave him, however briefly.

He insisted that I should go, so I did. I had a wonderful time. During the daytimes, I studied and wrote and immersed myself in the fantasy of becoming a full-time writer. It was not pure fantasy, because the course tutors were encouraging about my prospects. I began to hatch a plan to study for an MA in creative writing at the University of East Anglia, taught by the Poet Laureate, Andrew Motion.

It never happened. A few weeks after I returned from the writing holiday, I discovered I was pregnant. Paul and I were delighted, although a bit nervous about sharing our news with the rest of the world. We had both wanted to be parents even before we met, and now our dreams were about to come true.

54
Anna

From the start of my pregnancy, I relished the fact that I was carrying a child. Truth be told, I spoke and thought of little else.

Paul's family took the news well, considering the short time that he and I had known one another. My mother was delighted. My friends, my sisters, and my nieces and nephews were all pleased and excited too. For the first time in many years, perhaps for the first time in my life, I felt that I was truly and uncomplicatedly loved.

At work, the management were good to me, and let me take time off when I suffered bouts of sickness. In fact, as time proceeded the only cloud on the horizon was my health. I suffered from colds that turned into chest infections and had to take antibiotics several times. Otherwise, everything progressed smoothly. The first sound of the baby's heartbeat, the first scan, every health check I attended, were all fine.

I did not rest though. I pushed myself physically. I was conscious that I had not known Paul for long and felt it was important that I impressed him. So I kept on working and writing, while doing all the housework. I had moved into Paul's house in October 1999 and I cleaned the house daily, from top to tail. I hoovered, dusted, wiped the parquet floors downstairs, took all the net curtains down, washed and replaced them. I went on like this week after week, carrying out a permanent spring clean. I also practised my cooking, serving huge meals and puddings daily. I wanted to be the perfect woman for my new love.

Early in 2000, Paul and his father booked a last-minute skiing holiday. I didn't object, although I was unwell. I was taking a double dose of antibiotics for my latest chest infection and yet I still coughed and hacked my way through every night. I was seven months pregnant. Paul's mother invited me to stay for the week while the men were away. The heating broke at her house, but she insisted on staying there regardless. I desperately wanted to return to the comfort of my own home but I obediently agreed. I felt I had to be on my best behaviour with Paul's mum so I didn't dare take to my bed but instead spent the week visiting their relatives, trying to make polite conversation through my paroxysms of coughing.

My health gradually improved but I still took maternity leave at the earliest opportunity, eleven weeks before our baby was due. I was exhausted. The girls in my team at work held a baby shower for me and I was overcome by their kindness and beautiful gifts. The sight of a miniature hat and mittens brought it all home to me. It seemed miraculous that I was going to have a baby of my own, a tiny little person who would be wearing these lovely little outfits. I was truly blessed.

I felt really, completely happy. Paul and I started to buy things for the baby, a wooden cot, a pram, more tiny clothes. We were nesting.

Our home had one small double bedroom and a box room, which would be the baby's nursery. There was also a bathroom, a lounge-diner and a galley kitchen. Paul had decorated it all immaculately.

The baby's due date was a month away, at the beginning of May. One day in the shower, my waterproof radio began giving me messages, telling me to run away to London. I ignored it. I didn't wonder why

I was getting messages from the radio. The thought of mental illness didn't occur to me. Why should it? I was so blissfully happy.

I had been honest with Paul about my psychiatric diagnosis. I'd agonised over telling him, but our relationship became serious so quickly I knew I couldn't waste any time. I broke the news in the early weeks of our relationship, in the short month or two before I became pregnant. I was so frightened that I would scare him away that it took all the courage I had to say the terrible word 'schizophrenia'. To 'confess'. He seemed to understand, to my utter relief.

We attributed my two breakdowns to the fact that I had been smoking so much cannabis and had no security or stability in my life, and were both convinced that my problems were behind me. When the voices on the radio told me to go to London with my unborn baby I disregarded them and didn't consider mentioning them to Paul or anybody else. I blanked them out. They didn't happen.

I started to get cramps in my legs at night, which would wake me with a start. In the daytime when I climbed the stairs, my legs went numb. I accepted it all without complaint. Then one night, still more than three weeks before the due date of the baby, I woke thinking I was swimming in bed. I realised that I was soaking, cried out and woke Paul. 'My waters have broken!' I shouted. 'Get to the bathroom, quickly,' he yelled back. I dashed in there, trying to stem the flow and adjust to what was going on. Back in the bedroom, he was already phoning the hospital and packing my bag.

We left the house at 3.45am, Paul driving like a man on a mission, which I suppose he was. Everything slowed down when we arrived at the hospital. It had to, because there was no space in the delivery suite.

The nurses were relaxed. My contractions were strong, but first deliveries always take a long time, they said. They told me to wait in the day room. An hour later I was in terrible pain but the nurses were still sceptical. They had seen it all before, girls having their first baby, making a tremendous fuss. I had hours to go yet, they assured me. Perhaps days. Privately, I thought they were wrong, but I bowed to their experience.

At last, at 8.30, I was taken to the delivery suite. An hour later I was given pethidine, which magically stopped all the pain, and soon afterwards at 11.15am on 3 April, our baby was born. A girl. Anna. A millennium baby. A dream come true.

All too soon, the dream began to sour. The pethidine did stop the pain, but also made me lose touch with reality. I couldn't believe the medical staff when they said that Anna, who was a healthy weight of six and a half pounds despite her prematurity, had breathing difficulties.

I was still drugged from the pethidine and I felt angry and cheated as my daughter was wheeled away to the neonatal intensive care unit in an incubator on a trolley. I knew the doctors were lying and that there was nothing wrong with my daughter. Before I knew what was happening, she was hooked up to umpteen tubes and monitors, ostensibly to help her to breathe and stabilise her condition. It was a trick, to separate us.

Anna was kept in the Special Care Baby Unit for weeks. I was given a room nearby and Paul was allowed to stay with us. I was desperate to breastfeed Anna, but the nurses said I was unwell and urged me to rest. I didn't trust them. I couldn't sleep in case something awful happened to my baby while I was unconscious. I wandered out of our hospital room at all hours of the day and night to be with my daughter, to stand by her little glass cot and stare at her.

I insisted that Anna must only have breast milk. I had read all the literature and wanted to give my baby the best possible start in life. I expressed my milk, and the nurses gave it to her in bottles. My breasts were terribly painful, swollen and sore, but my baby was not allowed to suckle. Most of the time she slept sweetly on in her glass case.

Tests were carried out on Anna for all sorts of illnesses. The doctors called us to a meeting one day. My mother was visiting at the time and was present with Paul and I when we were told that they suspected Anna had Down's Syndrome. Normally, the doctors told us, it was possible to diagnose Down's immediately, but in a few cases the diagnosis was not certain. Chromosome tests had been carried out on Anna and the results would take three days to come back.

I was certain now that the doctors were trying to trick me. I felt confused, distraught. My baby was clearly perfect and I could not understand why anyone would suggest otherwise. I had been close to the edge for some time already, and now I had been tipped right over it, and was in an extreme condition of panic and fear.

I started to get visits in my hospital room from various nursing staff, doctors and social workers, but the penny did not drop. I had no idea that the psychiatric system was moving in on me once more. Meanwhile, the news came back that the chromosome tests were fine and there was nothing wrong with Anna. This was no consolation to me, since I had never believed in the possibility that anything was wrong.

Anna was moved to the ordinary hospital nursery and I tried to breastfeed her properly. I was so desperate to keep my baby close. But due to the stress and the fact that I was not eating or sleeping properly, my milk supply had dried up. I refused to acknowledge this, thinking it was another development in the plot against me. They wanted to wean Anna off my milk and take her from me.

I couldn't face the fact that my daughter was failing to thrive. She was losing weight, and the health professionals decided that the only way to protect her was to remove her from me.

Within a few days after my tiny Anna was given the all-clear from the battery of tests and ordeals she'd been through, my nightmare of losing her became a reality. I was taken by ambulance from the maternity unit in Poole to St Ann's Hospital under a section of the Mental Health Act. I had lost my baby.

55

St Ann's, The Third and Final Time

I was plunged straight back into the horror of St Ann's. At times I felt that I had never left the place, so vividly did the memories come flooding back. The treatment was as brutal as ever. Exactly ten days after my baby was born, I was literally dragged into the mental hospital. I believed I was Alice in Wonderland, I could feel myself growing and shrinking. I paused to vomit in the corridor and the staff forcibly restraining me stepped back momentarily, but as soon as I straightened up they began to haul me along again. Up some stairs to Merlin Ward. I had been sectioned for the third time.

In the hospital, once again, I was forcibly held down and injected more times than I could have counted. As before, my family visited, and some friends, and Paul's parents. This only had the effect of making me feel that I was humiliatingly on display. I was not well enough to communicate properly, but in my lucid moments I was acutely embarrassed by my condition. It was evident that Paul's family were shocked. I had told Paul about my mental health history but felt no need to broadcast it to his wider family. It was a shock for them to find out like this.

My moods and behaviour fluctuated. I was out of control, and publicly so. I was terrified of the place, the staff and the other patients. Worse than being scared for myself, I was fearful for Anna. What was happening to her, without me in Poole hospital? Gradually I became compos mentis enough to start taking the medication voluntarily, in order to stop having it forced into me. The worst of the regime receded but I was still in a state of constant alarm, shocked anew at the brutality of the hospital.

I was not the only person suffering. I watched as a young girl on the ward suddenly, inexplicably, broke down in tears. She was inconsolable. But that was all she was. Only sad. Not bad, not dangerous to herself or others. Yet within minutes of this outbreak of weeping the girl was offered medication. When she refused it she was immediately pounced upon and carried off by a group of nurses, screaming. It was like watching my 19-year-old self undergo the same treatment. I didn't need to see behind the closed door of her room to know that she was being forcibly injected with sedative drugs.

I wondered why the nursing staff didn't just leave her to cry it out. What were they so scared of? I feared for all these young girls, who should have had the whole of their future before them. I knew, because of this awful place, they might have no future at all.

After a week or two, Anna was discharged from the special baby care unit at Poole hospital into Paul's care. He brought her to visit me in St Ann's nearly every day. I slowly become reassured that she was well and safe, but I found it unbearable each time Paul and Anna went home without me. After some weeks I was moved to the Mother and Baby Unit at St Ann's, so that Anna could stay with me. There was more space there, and some peace, and it looked like things were getting better. Until, a few weeks later, I was sexually assaulted by a male nurse.

Peter was an ordinary-looking, pleasant-seeming nurse who worked on the ward. He told me he had a nine-month-old baby of his own at home. One lunchtime, I was in the dining room. I parked Anna's pram near a table and queued to collect my lunch,

261

glancing behind me at my baby to make sure she was safe. Peter was standing near the condiments and I nodded at him as I reached out to put some salt onto my tray. Suddenly, he grabbed my hand and placed it on his trousers, over his penis. I tried to pull away, but he held it there for a long moment. He had an erection.

I burst into tears and retreated as quickly as I could to my table, to my baby. I sat down to steady myself. I was crying like a baby myself, nose and eyes streaming. Peter was standing in the same spot, seemingly unconnected to the cause of my distress, pretending he hadn't noticed. I was leaking more and more snot, and I grabbed a napkin, blew my nose wildly on it, then crumpled it up and then (why? Why did I? But I did) I threw the soggy crumpled ball of tissue at the nurse, who drew back in shock. I was crying at him now, loudly. I grabbed Anna's pram and ran off down the corridor with her, back to the relative safety of the Mother and Baby Unit.

Another nurse came to find me. She was the nursery nurse in charge of the mother and baby unit. I was crying so hard I could hardly speak at first, but she insisted that I tell her what was wrong. When I did, she simply refused to believe me. 'He is one of my best nurses,' she kept repeating. But he is not, I wanted to scream. He attacked me! How could he be a good nurse?

I felt worse as the day went on and I gradually realised that nobody else believed me either. Even Mandy, when she visited, refused to listen to my account of what had happened. I remembered Betty, from Merlin Ward during my second hospitalisation, and how I and everybody else dismissed her claims of rape. Perhaps, I thought wildly, this was my punishment.

I couldn't understand any of it. At what stage, I wondered, did the fact that I was mentally ill morph into the universal conviction that I was a liar? I was powerless to do anything to change this.

Paul brushed the incident away, refusing to discuss it. Later, he told me he felt powerless to act since nobody at the hospital listened to him either, but I still felt let down, betrayed and scared. Shortly afterwards, Peter the nurse was appointed to be my key worker. It could not have been a clearer message. You are a liar, they were saying. We disbelieve your word against this man's, so much so that we are going to make sure he is the closest person to you in this hospital.

If I had ever trusted anybody in the hospital, I no longer could. Then disaster struck. The doctors decided that I was not capable of looking after Anna and she should be sent back home to Paul again. I was ushered out of the Mother and Baby Unit and sent back to Merlin Ward without my baby.

Another week or two passed. The spring was turning into summer and I was still in hospital. I was desperate. Paul still brought Anna to visit me, but months had passed since I first became ill and he had to return to work. This meant that our baby was looked after during the day by his parents and a local child-minder.

There was pressure on my relationship with Paul. This was partly to do with the reasons why I left the Mother and Baby Unit, and partly due to the fact that the poor man was scared silly. The girl he fell in love with was officially insane, sectioned in a mental hospital, held there under the Mental Health Act. This was like nothing he expected, unlike anything that had ever happened to him or anybody he had ever known. I was starting to wonder whether he would stand by me.

I missed my friends and family but still felt awkward and embarrassed when they visited. Day to day, time dragged interminably. There were times when I couldn't get any words out of my mouth, but other times when I couldn't stop talking. Moments when I was calm and lucid, and other moments when I felt completely panic-stricken. I longed to be in control of myself again, and most of all I wanted my little girl back. The situation seemed hopeless, for so long.

Finally, it was decided by the gracious, faceless doctors that I should be allowed to return to the Mother and Baby Unit with Anna. This time, I was determined that nothing would go wrong. I did everything that anyone asked of me. However stupid or contradictory or downright bossy any of the nursing staff seemed, I went along with them all. I also started to keep a daily journal, which I left open on the table in the unit lounge. I often saw nurses peering at it. This was fine with me, because I wanted them to know exactly what was going on in my head all the time. This way, there could be no room for misunderstanding, because I wrote far more clearly than I spoke.

There was one lovely Sister in the Mother and Baby Unit, called Ann. She often helped with Anna in the early evenings and one day she pointed out to me that this was the time when my mood often dropped, when I was tired. I was so grateful that she spoke to me as if I was normal and sane, merely going through difficulties like any other new mother.

Another male nurse, Sean, was sitting with me one evening as I looked after Anna. 'Are you having trouble weeing?' he asked. I was, as it happened, and I was startled that he knew about it. 'No,' I lied, embarrassed, and he let the subject drop. I pondered this later, and a small piece of a puzzle fitted into place. The inability to pee when I needed to was a problem that had affected me on both of my previous stays in hospital too. It was painful and had caused me considerable distress. Could it simply be a side effect of the psychiatric medication, I wondered. And if so, why had nobody ever mentioned it before?

Slowly, slowly, things became more stable. I was constantly supervised and had to take a lot of medication. But it gradually became evident that the ordeal which I had believed at times would never end was changing into a simple waiting game. I was allowed home, for a weekend at first, then a few days, and finally for a whole week at a stretch. At the beginning of July 2000, I was permitted at long last to return home, to be reunited with my baby daughter.

It was still a long uphill struggle. Paul and I had to get used to each other again, after our time apart. In reality, we had to get to know one another. It had been a whirlwind romance, and we'd spent such a short time together before Anna was born and we were separated.

I had to adjust to life with a baby. I was alone at home a lot in those early days, and I filled the hours by taking long walks with Anna in her pram, cooking her meals, and arranging her toys and clothes while she slept. I concentrated on the baby to the exclusion of everything else. Gradually I started to make new friends, other new mothers, and over the months I started to gain some confidence.

None of this was easy, but I had never found life easy. At least now I had people in my life to motivate me, a partner who loved me, our baby. I found happiness in small things in those days, like other first-time parents. I tried not to put pressure on myself. It helped that I was busy. Looking after a baby is a full-time job and I found this work fulfilling.

I did wish she didn't sleep so much. Anna slept all night and most of the day, and I wanted her to wake up and play more. At the baby clinic, where we congregated weekly to get our babies weighed and measured and talk over any concerns with the health visitor, the other mothers all complained about lack of sleep. They stared at me, clearly thinking me insane, when I confided that I missed Anna's company when she was sleeping. If this was insanity, I could live with it.

I was blessed to be Anna's mother. She was a

little treasure, good-tempered and bright. I started to attend a toddler group with her, and was bemused to find myself quickly surrounded by other cooing mothers, all besotted with my baby. 'She's so grounded,' one told me. I'd never heard the expression before and had to ask her what that meant. When she explained, I realised the woman was right. Anna was indeed grounded, completely sure of her place in life, sitting on a carpet in a new place surrounded by adoring acolytes, and remaining completely natural and unbothered by all the attention. My incredible child.

I discovered that having a baby made conversation much easier. I suddenly had something in common with other people, with other mothers. I read all I could find about parenting. I was determined that Anna should not grow up to be shy, so I made an effort to take her out as much as possible, braving other toddler groups, integrating into the local community.

A year passed, then we moved house. Our new home was a bungalow in a good area, walking distance from the local schools. We were lucky.

In the summer of 2001, Paul and I were married in a simple and sweet Registry Office ceremony, surrounded by family and friends.

We decided to try for a second child, and I was fortunate to get pregnant quickly. My GP was supportive, although some close family members thought I shouldn't risk having another child in case I broke down again. I knew that the converse was true, that becoming a mother had made me stronger, and that Paul and I were good parents. I knew instinctively that having another baby was the right thing to do.

My GP referred me to a psychiatrist to oversee

my mental health while I was pregnant. The doctor I saw was reasonable and kind. He suggested that I should take risperidone during the pregnancy, but I refused. He said it had been tested on rats and found to be safe, but I was unconvinced. Our baby was not a rat, I told Paul later, as I recounted the conversation indignantly. I no longer trusted the medics' opinions unquestioningly, certainly not when the health of my unborn child was at risk. It was not so long since psychiatric staff had told me that this same drug would not prevent me from conceiving.

Amy was born safely, and Anna rose to the challenge of being a big sister as if she'd been born for the job. I was advised to take risperidone after Amy's birth, and was disappointed but agreed reluctantly, because I did not want to risk another breakdown. I was told it would be safe to breastfeed while taking the drug, but I wasn't willing to chance this. Anna had thrived whilst mostly on bottled milk, Amy would have to do the same.

I continued to visit the same psychiatrist as an outpatient for some months after Amy's birth. He seemed sensible and solid, and I spoke to him openly. With his agreement, I quickly came off the risperidone. One day, he suggested that perhaps I had been misdiagnosed. He said that the things I had told him did not tally with the diagnosis of schizophrenia I'd been given all those years ago. Would I like him to look into getting the diagnosis changed?

Would I?! I was absolutely delighted at the prospect of a reprieve. During the two weeks until my next appointment with the doctor, I felt like a different person. A real, human person. One who had been unwell, but who was not permanently labelled insane. Not a schizophrenic but a Someone, with a future. A mother, above all.

When the appointment finally arrived, it was a disappointment. The doctor seemed to have changed. He regarded me differently, spoke to me tersely. He told me he had met with the 'Team' and now realised that the diagnosis of schizophrenia was definitely the right one, and it would stand. He refused to discuss the matter any further and I knew that I was defeated.

All I could do was put psychiatry to the back of my mind, carry on with my daily life and pretend that other people's opinions didn't matter to me. Most of my new friends, the other mothers I mixed with, knew nothing of my breakdown in any case. The few who did were not aware of my hospitalisation or the diagnosis. This meant that they took me at face value. Removal of the diagnosis would have changed my own opinion of myself but would not have made any difference to anybody else.

Some of my friends confided in me about things that happened to them soon after their babies were born, when they were hormonal and sleep deprived and some of these experiences sounded surprisingly familiar. One young woman told me she almost drove herself and her family, including her eight-week-old baby off the side of a motorway one day, deliberately. Another said that she was convinced she was being followed for months after the birth of her first child, and she had told nobody about it. I was astonished that these things happened to normal people.

I made a new friend when Anna was around two years old and Amy was a tiny baby. Rose was a mother of twins, and we attended a music and movement group together. Her children were Anna's age, and she was drawn to my lovely baby Amy. She invited me to her house one afternoon and while our children played, we chatted. Rose disclosed to me that she had bipolar disorder and that she'd had many breakdowns, the last after the birth of her twins.

The most amazing thing about this was that Rose was a professional, a child psychiatrist in fact. I told her in return about my mental health history and before long she suggested that we write a book together. She had a title ready. She wanted to call the book 'Mad Mothers'. I turned down her offer. I wanted to be known as a good mother, not a mad mother.

I was not the strongest of women and, with a toddler and a baby to care for, I found the long days and nights tiring, and struggled to cope with my emotions. But as I saw my children growing up, happy, strong and carefree, my confidence grew. I became more secure as I learned to relax in the loving home that Paul and I were building. My girls had so much faith in me and this made me determined to become all that they believed I was. I looked after myself physically, eating and resting as I needed, and I gradually became calmer. Routine suited me.

I read the newspapers daily. I had read The Independent since my student days, but when the girls were still young I changed to The Times. I read various articles on mental illness over the years, and often found reassurance in the stories of others. I discovered that I was not the only person in the world to have experienced psychosis and recovered. But I never met anyone in real life who admitted to a diagnosis of schizophrenia, and so I had the sense to keep my own story to myself. The last thing I wanted was to become a social outcast again.

I took Anna and Amy on various outings. Some of the members of the music group, including Rose, formed a reading group and we met at each other's houses once a month. Rose was open about her mental health diagnosis, and to my astonishment the other members of the group still respected her. I attributed this to her innate confidence and air of command, as well as the fact that she had a top job in a respected profession. Also, of course, she didn't have SCHIZOPHRENIA like me, but a mood disorder, which was more socially acceptable.

When Rose had a relapse and appeared at our subsequent book group meetings over-medicated and slow, nobody thought any less of her. I was the only person in the group who was unsettled by her illness, because it brought back anxious memories of my own experiences. I did my best to help Rose, though. She had been signed off work and was unable to drive, so I collected her from her house and took her for outings, coffee and walks.

On one occasion, while we were waiting for the ferry from Mudeford Quay to Hengistbury Head, Rose complained of the smell of the nearby lobster pots. 'The medication I am taking makes my sense of smell much more acute,' she told me, and another piece of the puzzle slotted into place. The smells I had experienced so strongly at St Ann's, which I had interpreted as olfactory hallucinations, more proof of my insanity, were mere side effects of the medication. If only I had known.

Another friend from our book group, Sarah, had daughters the same age as mine, and the six of us often went for walks together, pushing our buggies and chatting. One day she told me about a friend of hers from university, who'd had a breakdown and lost the ability to read. He'd been an avid reader, and was horrified. But Sarah told me that a psychologist had explained to him that this was a symptom of the way the mind works after trauma, and her friend had slowly recovered.

I couldn't believe what I was hearing. 'But the same thing happened to me!' I said. 'It was awful! I had a breakdown and I couldn't read, and that was one of the things that made me feel worst about myself.' Sarah hadn't said that her friend was hospitalised, and I didn't say that I had been, but it was a step forward for me to have confided in someone. Again, I was astonished to hear that a similar thing had happened to someone else. I knew other people had breakdowns, St Ann's was packed with them, but I honestly thought I was the only person in the world to have suffered in my particular fashion and it was extremely comforting to know that I was not, in fact, alone.

I wondered whether there might have been rational explanations for some of the other things that happened while I was in hospital. The electrical interference on television sets and the strong electric shocks I experienced when I was unwell, especially when opening and closing car doors, remained a mystery. I discovered that this experience (or delusion) was not unique to me, as I'd believed, but a common symptom of psychosis (the definition of psychosis itself removes some of the fear from the word, it means simply a

272

serious disturbance of the thought process).

Once, I saw a pink elephant moving across the sky outside the hospital, and I was convinced this was a visual hallucination, yet more evidence of my unhealthy mind. I looked at it in a new light now. Could it have been a hot air balloon, a blimp, some form of advertising perhaps?

And I had heard a voice, a clear voice in my ear when nobody was nearby, on two separate occasions. This was the thing I considered to be incontrovertible proof of my madness. It was the main reason I had given up hope for so many years, while I attended Hahnemann House. But it had happened shortly after I was let out of hospital, while I was still taking a lot of medication. Now, I couldn't help wondering if the voice might have also been a side effect of the medication.

It would really have helped if I could have understood some of these things better at the time, but I realised it was partly my fault for not confiding in the nursing staff. Why should they have informed me that urine retention, for example was a side effect of the medication, if I didn't confide in them that I had the symptom?

I'd been a victim of my own prejudice too. I would never have judged others as harshly as I judged myself, but I was terrified of 'madness' and those people I considered to be mad, and therefore dangerous, within the hospital. The language I used to describe St Ann's and the patients to myself, like loony bin, lunatic asylum, zombies and half-people was derogatory, and thinking in this way compounded my problems.

At Hahnemann House I'd been told that I suffered from self-stigma and I'd dismissed it. How could the nursing staff understand what it felt like to be

273

labelled schizophrenic? How could I hold my head up under this label? The idea of self-stigma seemed to lay the fault for any prejudice against mental illness at my own door, and I was not strong enough to deal with it.

So I had a childish understanding of mental illness and a great fear of it. I also saw my symptoms as evidence of my own weakness, and all these things held me back. But I had made some progress, and gained some insight, since becoming a mother. I knew now that I shouldn't try to bury all memories of my episodes of illness, because then it could creep back into my life undetected. I preferred not to dwell on it, and continued to construct the outward appearance of a balanced and 'normal' mother. Maybe one day I would believe in the myth myself.

I joined a local poetry group and attended their monthly meetings. I was still determined that my daughters should not suffer from shyness, so I made a concerted effort to be sociable in order to set them an example. I became garrulous, finding it easier to talk too much than to stay completely silent or wait for what others had to say and then react to it.

I still struggled with anxiety. I found the reading group and poetry group meetings excruciating. A panic attack often came on unexpectedly, blushes engulfed me. This terrified me but I persevered, steeling myself to attend the groups again the following month, and gradually it all became easier. Maybe my hormonal make-up was changing as I became older, maybe the adrenaline rushes were ceasing to create a response. Perhaps I was getting calmer, or wiser. It was a blessing and a relief to find that as I approached my mid-thirties I cared less about all sorts of things and was becoming more able to cope with life, in increments. I had to be, because I needed to set a good example to the children.

When Amy was two, I decided it was time to push our luck a little further. I was happy with my two girls, but I wanted another child. Paul was bemused by this, but acceded. When we'd first met we'd agreed on three children, or rather, Paul had said he wanted two and I claimed to want five, so we'd compromised on three.

The GP was not impressed. 'You're not going to put me through another one of these pregnancies, are you Louise?' she asked. I liked my GP. She was supportive and kind. For years she'd encouraged me to make regular monthly appointments, appointments that were double the usual length, and she'd patiently listened to me witter on in these sessions, and offered reassurance for my many anxieties.

She'd also referred me to the practice counsellor for two courses of six weekly sessions, and for years she'd signed the sick notes that entitled me to DSS benefits. She fussed over my daughters whenever I brought them into the surgery. In fact, when Amy was born she couldn't stop talking about how beautiful she was. 'You have to say babies are beautiful,' she'd said, 'But this one really is, Louise.'

I disregarded her comment about the new pregnancy. She'd made it in a lighthearted way, and I knew she was only referring to the extra paperwork that would be involved, the liaison with the Mental Health Team. It was me who would have to undergo the agonies of childbirth, and I already knew it would be worth it. It never occurred to me that I was blinkered. I was so secure in my conviction that my raison d'etre was motherhood and the more children I had, the better.

During my third pregnancy, I visited the same psychiatrist. I really wanted to breastfeed this time, and the doctor agreed that I could try. He prescribed a supply of risperidone to take with me to hospital when I went into labour but said I only had to take it if I felt it was necessary, after the baby was born. For once, I was to be trusted to be in charge of my own emotional wellbeing. The ball was in my court.

Scott was born quickly, like Anna and Amy, and with the minimum of fuss. However, after his birth things went awry. I was happily breastfeeding. I had gestational diabetes while I was pregnant, so had to stay in hospital for a few days after the birth to be monitored, to ensure that my blood sugar levels had returned to normal. But someone had alerted the staff to the fact that I had been mentally ill in the past. The doctors began to question me about my mental health. I insisted that I was well and happy, but they refused to believe me, and said that I had to start taking the risperidone, and bottle-feed Scott instead of breastfeeding him.

I was upset but took the medication because I couldn't risk being sectioned. Fortunately, the nurse in charge of the ward asked whether I would like to go home early and return for my diabetes test the following week. I leapt at the chance. Being told I was unwell and couldn't breastfeed my baby had brought me close to the edge, but thanks to the intervention of one old-fashioned staff nurse I was spared another breakdown.

The same nurse counselled me that it really made no difference whether I breastfed Scott or not. She had two children, she told me, and she had breastfed one and not the other, and nobody would ever be able to tell any difference from their health, or any other aspect of their well-being. I was still determined to breastfeed my baby though. When I got home, Paul agreed that I should go with the psychiatrist's original advice, stop taking the pills and start to breastfeed Scott again if I felt that I was able. It was the weekend, but when I contacted Dr Jameson on the Monday, he okayed this course of action. I had taken control of my own well-being, and it worked out very well.

Things settled and before I knew it Scott was six weeks old, perfect in every way. I was proud as punch. Anna was four and a half and had started 'Big School'. Amy was only two, and happy to be at home with the baby and I. Our little family was thriving. But my mum...

Mum was becoming more of a worry than usual. She was extremely unwell. She hated visiting the doctor, but one day she fainted at the checkout in Sainsbury's and I insisted on taking her to the GP.

I called Mum's doctor before I went to collect her. 'I am bringing my mother in to see you this morning,' I said. 'Whatever she tells you, the truth of the matter is that she drinks an inconceivable amount of alcohol, and this is almost certainly the cause of her ill health.'

Mum was a private person. So uncommunicative. Her drinking was surreptitious, underhand. There was nothing I would not have done or given for a sober mother and I believe all my siblings felt the same way. And yet we all loved and respected her, and we were in total awe of her abilities, her strength and courage. We respected her privacy and no matter how her alcoholism affected all our lives, none of us ever spoke to her about it. We talked to each other often, but never felt able to broach the subject with her. Even my strong, courageous sisters were not equal to the task of appearing to reproach our mother. None of us ever spoke about my mother's alcoholism to anybody outside the family either. Not our teachers, not anyone. This meant that I felt like a traitor speaking to her GP about it but I knew I had no choice, because her life could be at stake.

Mum and I sat down in the surgery together. The GP disregarded me and spoke directly to her. 'I have in your notes, Barbara, from two years ago, that you were drinking the equivalent of two bottles of Martini a day. Is that still the case?'

I was never more surprised in my life that when I heard my mother answer, 'Yes'. Apart from anything else, Mum didn't drink that stuff. Martini? She drank wine usually, and occasionally cider or lager. I cast about wildly in my head. I supposed she might have said Martini because she thought it sounded more sophisticated. Anyhow, more to the point, after all our years of enforced family silence on the subject of Mum's alcoholism, it appeared that her doctors had known about it all along. So why the hell hadn't they helped her tackle the problem?

Mum cried out in pain and misery from behind the curtain as she was examined by the GP. I sat on my side of the curtain, weeping for her silently and desperately, tears running down my face as I stared at my beautiful baby boy asleep by my feet in his little rocking car seat. When the doctor and my mother emerged from behind the curtain, the doctor regarded me gravely. 'I am sending your mother to have some blood tests. Come back with her in two weeks' time to get the results.'

I took Mum for the blood tests immediately. I was so proud of her. She looked a wreck, in every sense of the word, but she was so brave as the needle went into her arm. She was genuinely interested by how different the process is now compared to when she was a nurse. She seemed completely calm, chatting away happily to the nurse who carried out the procedure.

We were surrounded by other people with similar substance abuse problems; it felt to me as if we were caught in the midst of the entire spectrum of human misery. I found the experience difficult, but Mum had no problem keeping her dignity intact. She was a remarkable woman. Nobody would never equate her drunk persona with her sober one. The two were a world apart, and it puzzled me that they could be housed in the same body.

Mandy took Mum to the GP to get the results of the blood tests. I couldn't stand the misery of that office again. I had to think about myself and my new baby. But the news, incredibly, was relatively positive. By some miracle, there was no permanent liver damage. But the GP made it clear to my mother that if she continued to drink, she would certainly die. So, she stopped. Just like that. She was offered support, but she said she could manage it alone, and she did. The transformation in her health and her personality was literally astonishing.

For the first time in my life, I had a mother who I could talk to, and turn to for support. It felt like I had been reborn.

57
Cancer

Scott was two and a half, and my mother had been sober for nearly the whole of his life. Everything was good. But I was restless. I wanted more. One last baby. I pleaded with Paul. He was scheduled to have a vasectomy after Scott was born and I'd talked him out of it, not because I wanted another baby but because I didn't want Paul to suffer. It had left the way open for another child. 'Please. Please, please, please, please, please, please, please...' Of course, he caved in.

When Scott was born I was thirty-five. I would be thirty-nine by the time my next baby was due, and the extra years made a difference. The pregnancy was difficult and I was tired all the time. But I was relieved to find that now, expecting my fourth child, I was treated as a normal patient, although encounters with medical professionals still put the wind up me and I tried so hard to 'act normal' that they probably thought I was a little strange.

The pregnancy was hard, but relatively straightforward. Meanwhile, something else was badly wrong. I was eight weeks pregnant when my mum told me over the phone that she'd had a sore throat for several weeks. On further questioning it turned out to have been several months. Mum rarely confided in any of us about health matters so I knew she must have been in a lot of pain. I also had a sore throat and I advised her to gargle with TCP. 'It tastes horrid,' I warned, 'but it really does work.'

The next day, she bought some TCP, gargled with it and nearly collapsed from the pain. She went to the GP, who immediately referred her to the hospital. A week later, she had an appointment to see a consultant, which I knew meant that she was likely to be seriously unwell.

I was pregnant, with three young children to look after, and I felt overwhelmed. I called Mandy, who took Mum to the hospital. There, the staff made concerned noises and ran multiple tests. We were told that the results should be back in around three weeks.

Mum was seventy-two years old. The results, in fact, were back the next day. Mum had throat cancer, very advanced. She was given a date for an operation within a week. All of it happened so quickly, none of us had time to think. Mandy, Stephen, Jane and I were at Mum's bedside at 8am on 4 May 2007, as she was wheeled on a trolley down to the operating theatre. I held her hand, said cheerfully, 'See you later.' But in my mind and heart I was sure I was saying goodbye for ever.

It was nine long days before Mum woke up after the operation. I visited her in intensive care every day, staying for hours each time. When she finally woke, she had a hole in her throat with a large pipe threading down it. Her jaw was broken during the operation, and she had red raw stitches and scarring reaching right around her neck and head. She looked like Frankenstein's monster. She was on oxygen. She had a catheter. She was hooked up to a selection of monitors that bleeped and alarmed constantly. She was not allowed to eat or drink. And she could not speak. It was this fact that struck me hardest. My mother had the most beautiful, expressive, soft and cultured voice in the world. And it had vanished.

Still, she was awake, alive. Paul and I brought her a notepad and watched eagerly as she slowly formed the words to tell us how she was feeling. When she finally finished and turned the pad towards us, we were astonished to read, 'The doctors are trying to kill me.' It had not occurred to us that Mum might lose her mind.

She was allowed nil by mouth, she received all her nutrition from a glucose drip. She was extremely thirsty, but not allowed to drink. We were only allowed to put a damp sponge swab to her lips. She tried to suck the water out of it, like a child and glared at the poor lady in the opposite bed, who was allowed to have a proper drink.

Thank goodness, as the days went on, Mum gradually became lucid. Her progress was slow. She stayed in Poole hospital for months as one by one the various tubes and devices that supported her were removed. I'd longed to hear her voice again, but when the tube finally came out of her mouth and the hole in her throat was stitched together the sound that she made was not speech so much as rasps and creaks.

Anna and Amy were both at school, but little Scott only attended play school for a few mornings each week. I left him with Paul's mum and dad when I made my daily trips to the hospital to visit Mum. He wanted to come with me, but I was worried that he would be bored, and that the hospital was not a healthy environment for a two-year-old.

So, all through my pregnancy, Mum was unwell, and I was pregnant throughout her long convalescence too. When she eventually left the hospital, she was not well enough to go home alone, so she moved in with Mandy. I took her to Poole hospital every day for six weeks, for radiotherapy sessions, where I sat in the waiting room uneasily eyeing the other patients. I couldn't help wondering whether they were radioactive. The nurses in the department assured me that there was no threat to my unborn child, but I took nothing for granted.

My poor mum really suffered. She couldn't eat and could only drink protein shakes. Her voice returned, but it was a painfully hoarse, cracked, parody of speech. And when she was finally able to eat, all her meals had to be puréed.

When she managed to move back home, we were all very worried about her ability to cope. A short time after the move, she had to have new false teeth fitted because the shape of her jaw had completely changed. The new teeth caused her a lot of pain, but her speech became gradually clearer, and at last she could hold a conversation on the phone. Time and again, as the weeks and months passed, I was amazed by my mother's power of sheer endurance, her resilience throughout the whole awful process.

Luke was born. He arrived at 8am on his due date, 28 November 2007. He was born at Bournemouth hospital, in the water pool. He weighed close to ten pounds. And he turned out to be an angel baby, a bundle of energy and love. Having a fourth child was one of the best decisions I had ever made, Paul regularly told me. Incredibly, by the time of Luke's birth Mum had recovered a lot of her strength. I had doubted that she would even live long enough to meet him, and I will always remember the joy of her accompanying me to shop for his baby clothes.

At the time of writing, Luke is thirteen years old. Anna is twenty-one. My mother passed away last year from old age, peacefully in her own home.

I still cherish every moment with my growing family and understand that I am blessed. My children provide all the proof I need that there is a God in this world. I have been out of hospital and free from medication for many years, and I attribute this to the fact that I am secure, loved and fulfilled in my life.

At long last, I have peace of mind.

AFTERWORD

Childhood is the most precious of times, the most exciting and the most dangerous. My siblings were my companions on this journey, but I have written as little about them as possible, not because their lives did not impact on mine but because I do not want to compromise their privacy. I love you all.

As for my four amazing children, you are all bright and beautiful, and every day I am so grateful for your existence.

Once I only saw shame in my breakdown, but now I understand that things just happened the way they were meant to happen. I am proud of my survival, and I hope it will give encouragement to others.

I am passionate about ending the diagnosis of schizophrenia. Stigma destroys souls and this label is extremely damaging. Nobody can see into the inner workings of another person's mind or predict their future with any accuracy, and it is unreasonable and unfair for medical professionals to inflict the heavy burden of a dismal diagnosis or 'prognosis' upon another human being.

I now think of my three episodes of psychosis as manifestations of extreme anxiety. Anxiety is a problem I still struggle with at times, but it does not define who I am or what I am capable of. When I consider what happened to me and why, I realise that I became unwell because I lived according to the wrong rules. Instead of accepting that I was quiet and reserved, I tried to be outgoing and adventurous. The worst insult anybody could level at me for many years was that I was boring. I made my worst mistakes in life because I didn't want to be considered boring.

Cannabis was a major factor in my illness. If there is a single message that I would like any young person to take from this book, it is not to mess with recreational drugs, particularly that one. I recognise the first occasion that I smoked cannabis as the beginning of my long descent into madness.

As for coping with the aftermath of mental illness, apart from the side effects of the medication itself, a lot of the difficulty for me lay in how I thought of myself and of other 'mad' people. We need to cultivate understanding, to accept that every person will experience some degree of emotional distress during their lifetime and therefore not judge ourselves or others when those difficulties occur. Without stigma, including self-stigma, recovery would be much more straightforward.

In St Ann's Hospital during my third and final breakdown, a young student nurse sometimes used to visit me in my room. She would sit or stand quietly near me. One day, she picked up a bar of soap from my bedside table. 'What does this say?' she asked. I looked at the writing on the packaging. 'Simple,' I replied. She said nothing else.

I still think of that nurse, when my mind becomes complicated with petty worries about my work, or my friendships, or the lives of my children. When I start to panic about what would happen if my employers found out about the diagnosis, whether my children would be shunned if their friends found out about it. When I experience mood swings, or struggle to cope with the various ups and downs that life brings.

Simple. Calm.

In recent years I have attempted to learn as much as I can about mental illness, tried to find all the information available on the process of recovery and use it constructively, to prevent myself from becoming unwell again. I eat well, I sleep well, I take plenty of exercise, cultivate friendship and live a quiet and orderly life. And because I know that each of my three breakdowns happened six years after the last, the final six-year deadline felt like a milestone. I could assure myself that mental health problems would never get the better of me again. I have recently updated this book, and it has now been more than twenty years since my last hospitalisation. I am safe... I hope.

I want to pass on a message of hope within the pages of this book, to all those who are experiencing, or have experienced, mental illness and to the people who care for them or about them. Please believe me, there is hope. Take courage. Recovery is possible. Or, as my marvellous English teacher, Andrew Ransome, once told me, 'There's no such word as can't'.

And finally, I am lucky to have a wide and wonderful network of friends. Without your support over the years, the hard times would have been far more difficult, and the good times would not have been nearly as much fun. Thank you all for being there. I hope this book doesn't come as too much of a shock to any of you.

Made in the USA
Las Vegas, NV
05 October 2021

31761798R00157